DIGITAL IMAGING ESSENTIALS

TECHNIQUES AND TIPS FOR GENEALOGISTS AND FAMILY HISTORIANS

Geoffrey D. Rasmussen

2013

Middleton, Idaho

PUBLISHED BY
Geoff Rasmussen
Middleton, Idaho 83644

About the author

Geoffrey D. Rasmussen is the father of four budding genealogists. He graduated with a degree in Genealogy and Family History from Brigham Young University and has served as director and vice-president of the Utah Genealogical Association. He is a dynamic genealogy speaker on all forms of genealogy technology, and as host of the Legacy Family Tree webinar series, has spoken virtually to nearly 100 different countries. He recently received the Distinguished Presenter Award at the prestigious RootsTech conference in Salt Lake City. He has authored books, videos, articles, and websites, and develops the Legacy Family Tree software program. On a personal note, Geoff enjoys playing the piano, organ, cello and basketball. His favorite places are cemeteries, the ocean, and hanging out with other genealogists.

He met and proposed to his wife in a Family History Center.

Contact Geoff at Geoff@GeoffRasmussen.com.

Contents at a Glance

Contents

Foreword

If you are a genealogist with a computer, digital camera, or scanner I want you to love this book! If I could go back to the time when I started scanning my first documents and snapping my first digital pictures, I would do it with the knowledge of the techniques and principles that I have written in this book. Too many genealogists wish they could also turn back the digital clock! I have written this book so you can "do it right the first time," but if you have been at it for a while, you will benefit from the many tips and practical, real-life examples.

You will notice that it is written from my point of view and writing style – relaxed and down-to-earth, but to the point, with a little bit of dry humor throughout. I am also honest – if I like something – you will know it! but I will also let you know about what to watch out for.

In this day of the spell-checker and grammar verifier, I hope you will not notice anything out of order, but if you do, please let me know and I will get it updated for future revisions. The images and instructions in this book reflect the most up-to-date technology and this writing, but with its never-ending changes, some parts may be slightly different. Photoshop Elements version 11 and Picasa 3.9 were the latest editions at the time of this writing. Send me an email to my personal address of Geoff@GeoffRasmussen.com. I promise to read every email, but cannot promise to respond to every one. Oh how I wish I could use the clone tool to make a copy of myself sometimes.

Thanks to my wife, Tanya, and children Evan, Nathan, Braden, and Kaitlyn for letting me camp out in the office while I wrote this book. Thanks too for letting me use your pictures, you will all be famous! And thanks to whomever invented the digital camera and scanner, without whom I would not have a reason to write this book and ask for your money to buy the book.

I love genealogy and I love technology! I think I was born at just the right time. Thanks Mom…and Dad!

Preface

Twelve years ago I was asked by my younger brother to be his wedding photographer. Other than my fee (free) I had no professional qualifications to capture the memories of his special day. But I did have a digital camera. With it I could take up to 118 pictures! Just imagine all the money they would save by not having to develop a dozen rolls of 24s or 32s. In addition to my "professional" services, my gift to the newlyweds would be framed 8x10s of the best shots.

They got what they paid for.

When I returned home, I loaded all 118 digital pictures onto my computer. I chose the best ones, and printed each on my brand new color ink jet printer. To my horror, every picture looked like it was made up of a bunch of tiny squares. The printer was just fine. My computer was fairly new. My digital camera was the top-of-the-line. The problem lay in my non-understanding of *resolution*. You see, in order to take 118 pictures, and hoping to impress everyone at the wedding party, I changed the resolution on my camera to its lowest setting. I did not think for a moment this meant the resulting digital images would be made up of fewer pixels and, therefore have no ability to increase the size of the final product.

Oh how I wish now I would have read a book like this a few days before the wedding. If I had, I would have understood:

- What makes up a digital picture (lots of pixels)
- The importance of choosing the right resolution (dots per inch or dpi) settings on my camera or scanner software
- Which file format to use to safely preserve my digital images (jpg vs. tif)
- The importance of making editing changes only to a COPY of the digital image

Sounds like pretty boring, technical stuff, eh? (My wife is Canadian – have to impress her with my knowledge of 'eh' every now and then.) When these four concepts are understood, genealogists can safely preserve their original documents and old photographs – without regrets.

Over the years my personal and genealogical digital photo collections have grown to nearly 20,000 items, and now I have the desire to:

- Locate any media item (digital picture or video) quickly
- Share them easily
- Have access to my collections from any Internet-connected computer, tablet, or smart phone
- Ensure that I will never lose one of them

Through years of trial and error, learning from the experts, and staying on top of the latest technologies, I have developed a strategy that helps me accomplish my goals of digitizing, editing, preserving, searching, and sharing effectively and efficiently. Here is the strategy in its most elementary form:

1. Use a good digital camera or scanner to digitize family pictures and genealogy documents.
2. Use software that aids in the both the digitization *and* the organization of the digital media. Through this lens, I use Adobe's Photoshop Elements.
3. Use software to easily and inexpensively allow me to share my digital media with others through email, the cloud, and mobile devices. I use a combination of Photoshop Elements, Google's Picasa, and a number of online services.
4. Use multiple backup tools to ensure that my digital media will always be safe.

This book will:

- Teach what makes up a digital image
- Explain the three golden rules of working with digital images: 1) right resolution, 2) right file format, and 3) make editing changes to a copy of the original
- Show what to look for in a good digital camera and scanner
- Help you use your photo management software
- Explain the four steps of scanning a document or picture
- Teach how to import pictures from a digital camera
- Demonstrate how to repair your digital photos and improve their quality, while safely preserving the original
- Present an easy-to-use organization system for your digital media with the goal of finding anything in under a minute
- Give step-by-step instructions for using the two most popular photo management programs: Photoshop Elements and Picasa
- Describe and illustrate how to best share your pictures via email, CDs and DVDs, printing and mailing, Dropbox, and online via cloud technology
- Introduce a backup strategy to protect you from the day your computer quits

So if you are ready to take your digital pictures to the next level, go ahead … turn the page … and have fun!

A Digital Image is…

When the average genealogist hears the phrase *digital image* they first think of their digital camera. While this is 100% true – a digital camera does produce digital images (and digital movies too) – a scanner (flat-bed, wand, or even the popular Flip-Pal mobile scanner) also produces digital images. Therefore, an original will, a newspaper clipping, or even an old photograph can turn into a digital image.

Before digitization:

After digitization:

Digital images also come from the Internet. In fact, every picture that we look at online is a digital image. We sometimes download those images for our private use.

Whether we download an image or create it ourselves with our digital camera or scanner it is imperative to know what makes up a digital image so we know how to manipulate it later if needed. Digital images are made up of *pixels*! When we look at a printed picture we often do not notice the pixels, but when that image is digitized and we zoom in on it, we soon notice that the image is made up of hundreds or thousands of tiny dots. Zoom way in and you will find that each dot, known as a pixel, has one unique color. All of these pixels with all of their individual color variations, when put together make up a digital image.

Take a look at the images below. The one on the left is my favorite ancestor, Asa Clark Brown. Looks pretty good for an old photo, doesn't it? The one on the right is a zoomed-in image of his nose. Notice all the tiny pixels that make up this image. Each has its own color, and when all of these colorful pixels are put together and zoomed-in at 100%, they make up a nice image.

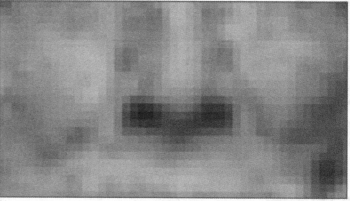

Now look at Asa's picture before I fixed the big tear at the top. The digital reason for the tear is that the pixels in the torn area have different colors than the rest of the digital image. If the different shades of red and brown had the same color variations as the rest of the background, it would appear as if there were no tear. Later in the book we will discuss how to easily fix the tear. For now, just remember that a digital image is made up of lots of tiny, colorful pixels.

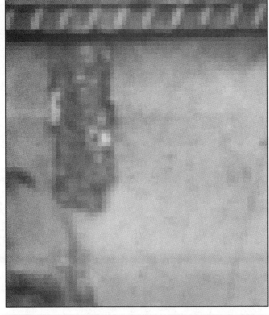

Before You Digitize

Before beginning any digitization project we must understand resolution and file formats. Without this knowledge we are doomed to visit the five stages of digital images grief:

1. Denial
2. Anger
3. Bargaining ("If only I had known when I first started…")
4. Depression
5. Acceptance

At a genealogy conference a few years ago an older gentleman visited with me and expressed his relief at finally being done with his two-year digitization project. He was beginning to insert the pictures into a book he was writing and was concerned about how they looked. He said that the pictures were too small and when he tried to enlarge them they appeared pixelated. I asked him a few questions to try to understand the situation, when he admitted that he scanned every picture at 72 dots per inch, chose to shrink them to 25% size, and saved the originals in the JPG format – all to save space on his hard drive. My response to him was not favorable as I explained the need for proper resolution and an archival-quality file format. There was no way to get the quality and size he needed without rescanning the originals. I suggested that he get another opinion to which he agreed. He came back the next day, appeared to have quickly gone through each stage of digital images grief, accepted the problem, and asked for guidance. We can avoid unnecessary duplication of our efforts by understanding resolution and file formats.

What will you do with the digital images?

To get started, you should have an idea of what you will do with the digitized images. Will you:

- Use them in a presentation?
- Publish in a book?
- Email to family?
- Enlarge to hang on the wall?

The answer to this question can help you determine how you should use your digital camera or scanner to digitize the document – sort of. But because you cannot possibly foresee all future uses for a digitized image, follow this 2-part golden rule:

1. Save the original digitized image at a high **resolution** (between 300-600 dots per inch)
2. Save the original digitized image as an archival-type **file format** (TIF) or be careful to only make editing changes to a copy of the original

Remember, you may get just one opportunity to digitize the image. For example, you are at your Aunt Clara's home in England. She will not give permission to take her original photographs with you for fear that they would get lost or never be returned to her. But she does give you permission to scan them while you are there. This may be your one chance to digitize. Someone who does not understand the golden rule may decide to save hard drive space by choosing a lower resolution (the resulting digital file will be smaller) and a file format like JPG that uses less room. These settings will be fine if all you want to do is view the digital image on your screen, but when you want to publish it in a book or enlarge it for framing, you will be out of luck. Therefore, understanding which resolution settings and which file format to save the digital image as is crucial.

Resolution

Resolution means different things for a digital output (screen) versus a printed output (paper). A document scanned at 300 dots per inch (dpi) will appear very large on the computer screen, and the quality will be pretty good when printed. The same document scanned at 72 dpi will appear much smaller on the screen, and the quality will be less when printed. However, the document scanned at either 72 dpi or 300 dpi will have the same dimensions when printed. You'll have to re-read that a couple of times! If you scanned a document at low resolution because you wanted to cut down on the file size, and then later you wanted to use the same image for a professional publication, you would not be able to unless the original was re-scanned at a higher resolution.

There are two categories of resolution:

<u>Printing resolution</u>. For images digitized and then printed, *resolution, to an extent, determines the quality of the image, not its size.*

If you will be printing your digital image to paper, the higher the resolution you choose when you create the digital image (via your camera or scanner) the better it will look when printed. The more dots in the picture the smoother and crisper the picture will look. There are limitations of course, depending on the type of printer you have, but for the most part – higher resolution results in a better-looking picture when printed. This is known as the *printing resolution.*

Scanned at 300 dpi.   Scanned at 72 dpi.

Above are two documents that I scanned and then printed. On the left, the document was scanned at 300 dpi. On the right, the document was scanned at 72 dpi. Notice that their printed size is identical. The 72 dpi document's quality is not as good, although it is difficult to tell in such a small graphic.

<u>Video resolution</u>. For images viewed on a computer screen, *resolution determines the size of the image*.

If you will be viewing the digital image on your screen, the higher the resolution you choose when you created the digital image the *larger* it will appear on your screen. For example, if your monitor's resolution is set at 1024x768 (a common resolution for your monitor, meaning you are able to view 1,024 pixels wide and 768 pixels tall) but the digital image has the dimensions of 4416 x 2480 you will not be able to view the entire image without saving the attachment and zooming out.

Above are two monitors both set to 1024x768 resolution. On the left, the picture was digitized at a lower resolution. On the right, the picture's resolution was much higher. You will not notice a difference in the *quality* unless you compare them as printed documents. But you do notice the difference in *size*.

So if you will be creating a digital image *only* to share it with someone in an email, then selecting lower resolution (100 dpi) at the time of digitization is fine. But if a month later you decide you want to print the image on your printer or upload it to a photo printing service to have it professionally printed, it may not look good. It may appear pixelated. Therefore, follow the golden rule by choosing between 300-600 dpi.

My guidelines

As a general guideline, when scanning a document to become a digital image, I use the setting of 300 dots per inch and save the image as a TIF. If I am scanning a one-of-a-kind, rare, original document, like my family's bible, I use the setting of 600 dots per inch and save as a TIF. Although my current printer may not be able to take advantage of the higher dpi setting, other future technology will likely be able to.

In conclusion – digitize now with the future in mind.

File Formats

The next rule to understand before your digitization process begins is which file format you will use to save the original digitized image. If the digital image comes from your digital camera, the choice is usually already decided for you as most cameras only produce JPG images. If you are using a scanner, immediately after you make your scan, when you are saving the original, you have a choice as to which file format to use.

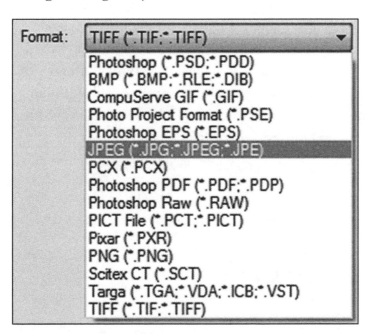

The two most popular file formats are JPG and TIF. Each has their place in our digitization plans but we must understand when each is good to use.

The JPG (stands for Joint Photographic Experts Group) is the most popular format for images because of its smaller file size and compatibility. When you choose to save your digital image in this format, it uses what is called a lossy compression method to keep the file size down. This is great for sharing images online or via email because the file size is smaller, and thus easier to share. The major downside though is that if we are not careful, when we make an editing change to the original (cropping, repairing, adding color – any editing changes) AND we re-save the image, the image gets even more compressed.

Non-technically, this means that some of the pixels that made up the original get squished out – or compressed. Think about what happens when you make a photocopy of a photocopy of a photocopy. Each subsequent copy loses quality until you can barely make out what the copy is supposed to be. The same thing happens when saving and re-saving and re-saving a digital image that has been saved as a JPG.

Do not become depressed about this though – you can still use JPG as your preferred file format as long as you *make any editing changes to a copy of the original*. For example, let's say that you scanned a family photograph and immediately saved it as a JPG. Here's the file name you chose:

> family.jpg.

Then you noticed that the image needed to be made a little brighter, and so using the editing techniques you will learn in this book (keep reading...) you brightened the dark areas. To retain these changes, you needed to re-save the image. The moment you clicked the save button the image got compressed. The next time you view it, you may or may not notice that the image is a little more pixelated. But then you notice another problem – a minor scratch – and so you use the clone technique to fix it. Then you click the save button again. Once again, the image gets a little more compressed, or, some of the pixels that made up the original get squished out again. Eventually it will be easily noticeable that your digital image is not what it once was.

Here's the golden rule for working with digital images – especially with those in the JPG format:

> Make changes to a digital image to a *copy* of the original.

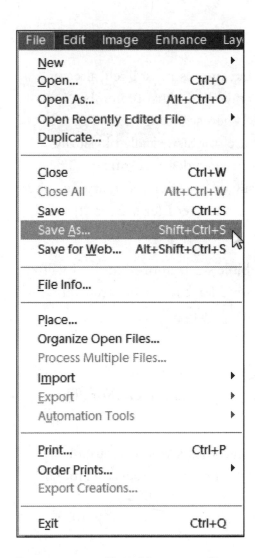

So, use your digital image software to make a copy of family.jpg. Or, using your Windows Explorer, just follow these steps:

1. Right-click on the image and select Copy.
2. Right-click in an open space and select Paste.

Notice that you now have two images – family.jpg and family-copy.jpg. If you wish to make editing changes, do it to the copy.

Even better, save the original file in the TIF format. Experts say that the Tagged Image File Format, or TIF, is the best format for archival purposes because it will not lose image quality when re-saved. Basically, TIF does not use a lossy compression process, but this results in large files. So while the file size of the family.tif image could be 10MB, when saved as a JPG the file size could become 1MB.

So when do we use TIF and when do we use JPG?

If your digital images are created from your camera, this question is most likely already decided for you as most cameras only produce JPGs. No problem – just remember to make a copy of the original if you plan to do any editing. When scanning genealogy documents, I personally choose JPG for documents that are not historically physically valuable, such as a copy of a recent newspaper clipping or even a death certificate. The reason for this is that these documents can usually be easily relocated if necessary. In other words – if I lost the digital image of the death certificate, I could reorder it from the vital statistics department.

However, when we are talking about my Brown family's bible – a one-of-a-kind – I will take the extra care by saving its pages as TIFs. Then I know I have a terrific, archival-quality digital file of the bible in case I ever lose the original pages.

I am often asked, "if I have a JPG, can I re-save it as a TIF?" The answer is yes, you can save it as a TIF and should if you plan on making editing changes, but you will not gain any *more* quality by doing so. But if you make any editing changes you can sit comfortably knowing that you will not lose quality.

These are not your only choices of file formats, but for genealogists who care about preserving their photos and documents there really are not others that deserve as much attention.

Scanners, Cameras, Wi-Fi, Mi-Fi, and Eye-Fi

Among the thousands of choices of scanners and digital cameras available how does the genealogist decide which to use? You already know that you need to have good resolution and select the right file format. I will be up front with you – probably every brand new digital camera or scanner in the store is good enough for what you want to do today. But will it be good enough for the future? Again, in most cases they probably will, but as technology advances, it will be able to take better advantage of the features in the higher end cameras and scanners, so my personal preference is to get the best out there. Usually, in this field, you get what you pay for. So how do you know what you need? Below are some ideas to consider.

Which Scanner?
The answer to this question may depend on what your needs are now and in the future.

What do you need to scan? If you will only be scanning black and white documents, then look for a scanner that meets those needs. But do not limit yourself today because your needs may change in the future. You will certainly be scanning old photographs and genealogy documents, and every brand new scanner will do a fine job. But what about negatives or slides? Make sure your scanner has a negative or slide adapter.

How large are the documents and photos you will scan? Any 8x10 flatbed scanner will work, or even the Flip-Pal mobile scanner is large enough to scan 4x6 images, but what about those legal-sized documents like the copies of pension records I made at the National Archives? Unless you know how to use stitching software (you will if you read to the end of this book), it is easier to have a scanner that scans up to 11x17. The larger the scanner, however, the less portable it becomes. This is where the Flip-Pal mobile scanner comes in. Although it only has a scan area of 4x6, it will let you take multiple scans, and its software stitches the pieces together. It is lightweight and runs on batteries. It works independently of your computer, meaning, you do not have to attach it to your computer to initiate the scan. When you are done scanning, you simply insert its SD (Secure Digital) card into your computer to transfer the images.

All-in-one

I actually use a combination of three scanners for different purposes. First, I have an all-in-one which I use primarily as my printer, but it also gives me the ability to scan, fax, and copy. I love it as a copier and printer. I never fax anything but it is there if I need it. It has a sheet feeder but do not use it for your historical documents and photos. I do use it to scan multi-page contracts and other documents that I want to quickly scan – way faster than scanning one page at a time, but again, I only use it for non-historical documents. So there really is a place for an all-in-one unit. Mine happens to be a 2-year-old Canon imageCLASS MF4350d which prints only in black and white (wow I have saved a lot of money in ink since I got rid of my color laser printer) but it scans in color. I do not use it as my scanner for my old photographs because simply, my dedicated photo scanner is designed specifically for that.

Flat-bed

My flat-bed scanner is an Epson Perfection 4490 Photo scanner. I have had it for a few years and its specifications still exceed what I need it to do today. Its bed allows me to scan up to an 8.5"x11.7" surface which has been adequate most of the time. It is large (takes up desk space) and heavy (not very portable), but it is designed specifically for scanning photos and documents. It does have to be plugged in to the wall outlet, which again makes it less portable. It also has to be plugged into the computer – it does not capture images on its own – it requires the use of scanning software on the computer to initiate the scan.

Flip-Pal mobile scanner

Finally, I own a Flip-Pal mobile scanner, although I do not use it as often as the other two. I will bring my Flip-Pal to libraries and archives that permit its use (even the National Archives in Washington D.C. permits them). It is very portable. Just be sure to have a spare set of batteries. They recommend that you use nickel-metal hydride rechargeables (abbreviated NiMH) and say that you can get up to 450 scans before the batteries need to be recharged. More on this later on.

Wand scanners

Some people like the wand scanners. Honestly I do not have a lot of experience with them. The first and only one I owned was back in 1994 at college. Everyone in the dorm thought I was the biggest techno-geek because they had never seen such a thing. The way it works is that you slowly move the wand over the photograph/document as it does its digitization. They have improved tremendously over the years and are very portable. Some archives and libraries do not permit its use because it requires that the scanner touch the document. Because you also have to move the scanner while touching the document, there is the possibility of damaging the original if you are not very careful.

If you are still on the fence while browsing the office store or website, look to see what software comes with the scanner. If it comes with something like Photoshop Elements, AND it has the specifications you want – get it! This software on its own runs between $60-100. As you will read later, you do not need to purchase software – your computer already likely has its own simple photo editing and management software, but in this realm, you also get what you pay for.

For more reading, see "How to buy a scanner" at http://www.pcmag.com/article2/0,2817,2355771,00.asp and "Top 5 Photo Scanners" at http://www.pcmag.com/article2/0,2817,2362752,00.asp.

What to look for in a digital camera

It took my aunt many years to overcome her bias against digital cameras. I do not think it was until stores stopped carrying and developing film that she switched. Digital cameras do amazing things and have improved so much that nearly any camera you look for at the camera or tech store will be good enough. I will admit that I am not a professional photographer, nor do I know everything about this field, but in my experience, there are a few things that I specifically look for in a new digital camera.

Resolution – each digital camera has the ability to adjust the resolution from low to high. If you will be taking pictures with the intent of sharing the photos online or in an email, using a lower resolution is fine, but because you will not know all of the future intended uses for your pictures, I recommend using the highest resolution possible. Back in 2000, my top-of-the-line digital camera's highest resolution was 3.3 megapixels and I paid $850 for it. I purchased it just three days before my first son was born. He ended up being in the intensive care unit for the first two weeks of his life, and for the first day or so, the only way my wife could see him was through the use of this camera. Regardless, today a 3.3 megapixel camera belongs in a museum of ancient history. Here is a chart from http://cameras.about.com that illustrates the resolution needed for various print sizes:

Resolution	Average quality	Best quality
0.5 megapixels	3x5 in.	N/A
2 megapixels	8x10 in.	3x5 in.
4 megapixels	11x14 in.	5x7 in.
6 megapixels	16x20 in.	8x10 in.
8 megapixels	20x30 in.	11x14 in.
10+ megapixels	25x40 in.	13x17 in.

Other charts are similar, but all agree that the higher the megapixels, the better the quality in the printed picture. 16 megapixel cameras today begin at around $100. While your printer may not be able to take advantage of printing to 13x17, you can upload your photos to various sites that can take advantage of the extra resolution. Resolution counts – the higher the better, but the more space each picture takes on your hard drive.

Zoom. Digital cameras have varying optical and digital zoom settings. When deciding, always go for the camera with a higher optical zoom. Optical zoom uses the lens of the camera to bring the object closer. Digital zoom really does not matter. It is the same as zooming in on the digital image with your digital image editing software. You will notice that the more you zoom in with the digital zoom the more pixelated the image becomes. If given the choice between a camera that advertises 5x optical zoom and 15x digital zoom versus a camera with 10x optical zoom and 5x digital zoom, go for the latter. You will have much more flexibility and enjoyment with your camera and the resulting pictures.

JPG vs TIF. If you will be doing a lot of editing of your digital images, remember that TIF is the best format to use, unless you remember to make a copy of the original before editing. If you can remember to make a copy, then it does not really matter if the camera has a TIF setting or not. Cameras with it usually are more expensive, and you will not be able to take as many pictures on your storage device.

Wireless. Imagine snapping a picture and having it automatically transferred to your computer at home, your online photo album, and emailed to your mother. Your family or friends can join you on your vacation without you having to put up with them. If the digital camera has wireless capabilities built in, you are that much closer to making this happen.

Keep in mind that the camera will not have Internet built-in, just the ability to *use* Internet tools *if*:

- the camera has the wireless capability
- *and* you are within a wireless network
- and can connect to the wireless network

That might seem like a lot to keep straight. Here's an example – you are on vacation in a city which has free wireless access everywhere. Using your camera, you can connect to the open Wi-Fi network. Using either the camera's built-in tools, or an Eye-Fi card (sold separately), after snapping a picture, you can have that picture sent to your Facebook, Picasa, Flickr, other accounts, or even your computer.

You can still go wireless with your digital camera (or even the Flip-Pal mobile scanner because it too uses an SD card) even if it is not built in. All you need is a different kind of SD card (this is the memory card that you insert into your camera that stores the digital images) called an Eye-Fi card. Stick the Eye-Fi card into the SD card slot and snap away. There is a little setup involved on your computer first, but depending on your settings, once you are within a wireless network range and your camera is turned on, the Eye-Fi card begins transmitting your digital pictures to your computer at home or to your favorite photo sharing site.

My parents live over 1,300 miles away, and do not get to spend many holidays with us. Imagine this – Christmas morning comes and I snap a few dozen pictures. As I snap the pictures, they are instantly uploaded to my Picasa web albums account, to which I have given my mother access. She receives an automated email notifying her that I have added new pictures to my album, and she is able to watch the new pictures arrive. Wonderful technology!

If you are snapping pictures in an area without access to a wireless network, consider purchasing and bringing your mobile broadband card with you. Though not inexpensive, these cards, like the MiFi card from Verizon, act as mobile Wi-Fi hotspots. In other words, you can bring access to the Internet with you – for a monthly fee of course. This works well when you are at the cemetery snapping away. With your MiFi card in your pocket, and your Eye-Fi card in your camera, your pictures are automatically uploaded to your computer, Facebook, genealogy society's Dropbox folder, or your favorite photo sharing site.

The same holds true with the Flip-Pal mobile scanner. Simply remove the included SD card, insert the Eye-Fi card, and after scanning your image/document, it gets wirelessly transmitted to your desired location. Although I have not heard of it being done, imagine the possibilities of a genealogy society working together. They have a couple of people scanning documents at the courthouse with their 1) Flip-Pal mobile scanner, 2) Eye-Fi card, and 3) wireless access. As the documents get scanned, because of how they set up the Eye-Fi settings, the digital images wirelessly transfer to the society's Dropbox where everyone now has access. The possibilities seem endless.

The best thing about the Eye-Fi Pro X2 model (there are a few models, this is the most powerful) is that it includes the ability to geo-tag each picture. This embeds the latitude and longitude information into the image's metadata which allows you to view all of your photos by location.

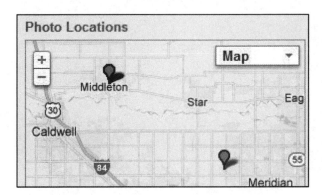

Visit www.eye.fi for more information. Excited yet?

Image Stabilization. Newer technology, image stabilization helps the camera reduce blurry photos from camera shake. Most new digital cameras come with this.

Tripod vs a steady hand. One last thing to consider is purchasing a tripod for your camera. Even my son's $20 digital camera has the ability to connect to a tripod so locating a digital camera without this ability would be difficult. I use a tripod for taking those self-timed photos of our family *and* for taking pictures of documents. Without a steady set of hands, it is more difficult to take a picture of a document with text that needs to be focused.

For more reading, see "How to Buy a Digital Camera" at http://www.pcmag.com/article2/0,2817,2403874,00.asp and "The 10 Best Digital Cameras" at http://www.pcmag.com/article2/0,2817,2369450,00.asp. Are you falling in love with PCMAG.com yet?

Photo Software

Before you can start scanning, your computer needs a way of communicating with your scanner. In addition to connecting the *hardware* (connect the USB cable from your scanner to an open USB port on your computer), you also need to install the driver that came with your scanner. A driver is the technical term for the software that permits the two to communicate. Just follow the step-by-step instructions that came with your scanner to get it set up. There is really no easier way to say it than that. Since some driver software comes on a CD, while others are downloaded from the Internet (either manually or automatically), the instructions, usually called the "Quick-Start Guide" that came with your scanner is your best resource to get started.

In addition to the driver, you will also need photo editing software – like Photoshop Elements or Picasa. When you tell the software to start scanning, it initiates the driver software, you make a few choices on how you want to scan, and the digital image is then created and appears on your screen.

Now that that boring stuff is out of the way, let's talk about which photo editing software to use. There are dozens, and probably hundreds of them available, both free and paid. The two most popular software programs for Windows computers (disclaimer – I'm not a Mac guy so cannot speak to it) are:

- Adobe's Photoshop Elements
- Google's Picasa

Photoshop Elements is Adobe's consumer edition of their flagship program – Photoshop. Photoshop is what many professionals use and has a whole bunch of extras that we amateurs would not know what to do with. Photoshop Elements is perfect for the consumer and has just the right combination of features and ease-of-use qualities to make it popular among genealogists. It functions as both a photo editor and a photo organizer. Learn more at http://www.adobe.com/products/photoshop-elements.html. It is usually priced between $60-$100US.

Picasa is Google's popular photo software, and like Photoshop Elements, it functions as both a photo editor and organizer. Although not as robust as Photoshop Elements (you do get what you pay for sometimes) it works just fine for most beginners. It is very intuitive and easy-to-use, probably more so than Elements, and makes synchronizing and sharing your pictures via the web very simple. Learn more and download for free at http://picasa.google.com.

Other popular photo software include, but is not limited to:

- Adobe Photoshop Lightroom - http://www.adobe.com/Lightroom
- ArcSoft's PhotoStudio – http://www.arcsoft.com
- Corel PaintShop Pro – http://www.corel.com
- CyberLink PhotoDirector – http://www.cyberlink.com
- GIMP - http://www.gimp.org/
- IrfanView - http://www.irfanview.com/
- Serif PhotoPlus X5 Digital Studio - http://www.serif.com/photoplus/
- Windows Live Photo Gallery - http://windows.microsoft.com/en-US/windows-live/photo-gallery-get-started

If you want simple photo editing and do not want to install software, there are some online sites like:

- Adobe Photoshop Express - http://www.photoshop.com/products/mobile/express
- Fotoflexer - http://fotoflexer.com/
- LunaPic - http://www.lunapic.com
- Pixlr Editor - http://pixlr.com/editor/

Personally, I use a combination of Photoshop Elements and Picasa. I use Elements for its simple, yet powerful editing features and its superb organization of my collections. I use Picasa for its remarkable ability to selectively share my photos online with those to whom I have given permission. I also use a few apps to access my photos in the cloud via my smartphone and tablet. More about this later on.

For more on comparing photo editing and organizing software, visit www.pcmag.com and www.cnet.com.

How to Import from your Scanner or Camera

Now that you have the perfect scanner, it is connected to your computer, and your software is set up, it is time to make your first perfect scan. Here is the summary of the process.

4 Steps to digitizing a photograph or document using a Flat-bed scanner
1. Open your photo editing software (Photoshop Elements, Picasa) and initiate the scan.
2. Set your scanning preferences.
3. Scan.
4. Immediately save the original image.

Step #1 – Open your photo editing software (Photoshop Elements, Picasa) and initiate the scan.

Before powering on your scanner and placing the picture or document on the scanning bed, check the bed and the photo for any lint, dirt, or smudges. You can use canned air to blow off the dust on the photo or bed, but probably do not use it for old photos that could crack. Now, carefully position your photo or document on the glass just as you would with a photocopy machine. Next, close the cover and launch your photo editing software.

Photoshop Elements

In the Editor (not to be confused with its Organizer), go to File > Import and click on the desired scanner. Piece of cake. Done with step 1.

Picasa

Click on the Import button (upper left) or go to File > Import from and click on the desired scanner. Piece of cake. Done with step 1.

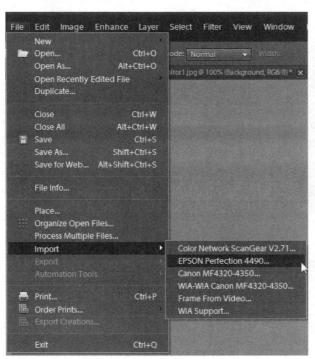

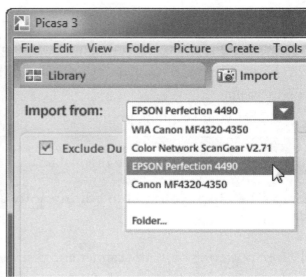

Step #2 – Set your scanning preferences.

This is the part where my illustrations below will probably be a little different than what your screen looks like – it depends on the driver software that works with your scanner. But the principles are the same. At the very least, your preferences screen should give you the ability to adjust the image type (color, grayscale, black&white), and resolution (dots per inch). If not, look for a *customize* or *advanced* button. In the example below, its default is "Full Auto Mode" where the decisions are made for you. You can change this to either Home Mode or Professional Mode which give you more control of the scanning preferences.

Full Auto Mode:

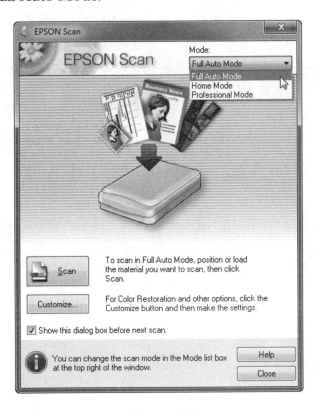

Home Mode:

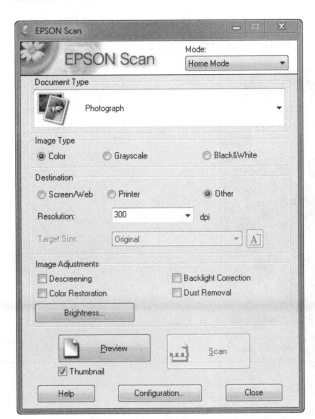

<u>Image Type</u>. Select Color, even if the photo is black and white. You will have more customization flexibility later on, and can always convert the photo back to grayscale if you want, but not the other way around.

<u>Resolution (dots per inch)</u> This is your last chance to do it right! Higher is better. Remember, you do not know what future technology will be able to do with more resolution. Scan for the future. Use 300 dpi for most originals and 600 dpi for those you really care about.

With any other preference – be careful. If, for example, you choose the Color Restoration, Unsharp Mask, Dust Removal, or others at the time of scanning, you are altering the original scan. You will not be able to get back to what the original picture looked like if you want to. As you have previously learned, digitize the original, save a copy of it, and then make any editing and clean-up changes.

Some other preferences may include:

<u>Descreening</u>. When this check box is selected, moiré patterns are automatically removed from scanned images. This increases the scanning time. This would be a preference that I would turn on before scanning a newspaper or magazine as it is not easy to adjust the moiré problems afterwards.

The example below of my great-grandfather's obituary shows the scanned newspaper without (left) and with (right) the Descreening option turned on:

Color restoration. When the Document Type is set to Photograph, Positive Film, Color Negative Film or B&W Negative Film and this check box is selected, color faded image is restored automatically. If you select this option for normal color image, the image is scanned with abnormal color.

Dust Removal. When the Document Type is set to Photograph, Positive Film, Color Negative Film, or B&W Negative Film and this check box is selected, dust on the original is automatically removed from scanned images.

Unsharp mask. Select this check box to improve the image sharpness. When you click the + mark, the Level list box appears. You can select one of the following level settings of the Unsharp Mask: Low, Medium, or High.

Grain Reduction. When the Document Type is set to Film, Film (with Film Holder), Film (with Film Area Guide) or Film (from Auto FilmLoader) selecting this check box reduces the degree of film surface roughness thus caused in using high-speed films or scanning with a high resolution.

Backlight Correction. Automatically adjusts the scanned images, originally taken in a backlight condition, so that the shadowed parts become brighter.

These preferences are independent of your photo editing software, meaning, you will see the same preferences screen whether you use Photoshop Elements, Picasa, or others.

Step #3 – Scan

You are halfway done! Click the Preview button. Your scanner will do a quick preview of the picture. Make sure that in the Preview pane it looks straight, there are no major unnecessary smudges or dirt, and if necessary, move the crop/selection lines so that you have selected the entire picture, and nothing more.

Click the Scan button. Depending on your preferences, it may take from a few seconds to more than a minute to complete the scan. If this is your very first scan, congratulations, you are almost done! I remember when and where I was when I scanned my first picture ever. I was in my dorm room as a college freshman back in 1993. But I digress.

Step #4 – Immediately save the original image

Before doing anything else, save the original:

Photoshop Elements

1. In the Editor, go to File > Save.
2. Change the folder to which you will save the picture (more on this in the Organizing section of this book).
3. Change the Format to TIF. If you want to use JPG, that's fine. Just remember in the future to never make edits to this file – make them to a copy of this file.
4. If you want the picture to appear in the Photoshop Elements Organizer (collection of all your pictures, also discussed later) make sure that "Include in the Elements Organizer" is selected.
5. Type a unique file name.
6. Click the Save button. Do not yet make any editing changes.

Picasa

1. Change the folder to which you will save the picture (see the Import To area in the lower left of the screen).
2. Choose the Folder title.
3. Click the Import All button (or click once on the picture and then click the Import Selected button).

If you are following the Picasa steps notice that there is not an option save your new digital image as a TIF or any other file format for that matter. Also, the resulting JPG Quality (on a scale of 1-100, with 100 being the best) is 85. You do not get the choice to name the file – by default the newly-created digital image is given the file name of image0.jpg. If you study the Picasa forums, the most frequent response given to those who question this is, "do not use Picasa to scan your photos, use anything else. Picasa is really made to import and organize your existing pictures." So I am not trying to be the bearer of bad news for Picasa fans, just the bearer of what is currently possible with technology. My suggestion would match that of the suggestions on the Picasa forums – use a different photo editor program to do the original scanning of your photos and documents. Keep reading though…you will learn why I could not live without Picasa soon.

Creating a unique file name

Before discussing the step-by-steps for using the Flip-Pal mobile scanner or your digital camera, a little more about saving the original image is needed. Before clicking the Save button (step 4), you are required to give the new file a name. This is often a difficult decision. In the olden days (15 years ago or so) file names had a limit of eight characters and so we had to be creative. For example, the wedding picture of David Brown and Clara Crosby could be named as:

dcbcec.tif
browndc.tif
bdavid1.tif

Today file names can be as long as 255 characters. With this knowledge, here are my two golden rules for coming up with a good file name:

1. <u>Long, more descriptive is better</u>. You might have a specialized system that works for you, where different parts of the file name represent different things. For example in this file name, bc1920john1862.jpg, the b stands for Brown, the c stands for Census, 1920 represents the year, John stands for, well, John, and 1862 is the year John was born. This syntax could work really well for you. But when you pass along your digital file collection to your children, will they understand it just as easily? 255 characters gives you flexibility to name this file something like "Brown, John, 1862 – 1920 census.jpg" This is much more descriptive and easier for others to make sense of it.

2. <u>The file name should be unique</u>. When I began scanning my family's old photographs years ago, I created one folder for each year. Within that folder I saved the images for that year. So the first picture of 1975 that I scanned I named 1.tif, the second 2.tif, and so on. Then I created the 1976 folder, and began again with 1.tif, 2.tif, 3.tif. You get the idea. The problem with this is that now I have different files in different folders with identical names. Although they are located in different directories, this can have unforeseen consequences later on. One way of ensuring that every digital image's file name is unique is to assign it a date. The file name of the picture of me on the day of my birth is called 1975-08-13-0001.tif, where 1975 is the year, 08 is the month, 13 is the day, and 0001 is the number of the picture for that day. Although this method does not describe the contents of the picture (which really is the Organizer's job anyway), it easily follows a naming system that will not easily get confused with itself.

Next time you import photos from your digital camera, take a look at their file names. Your camera is set up to follow this golden rule. Although the resulting files are named pretty cryptically (ie: DSC-1003.jpg), each file is unique. When importing your photos using Photoshop Elements, look for the option to rename the files based on their date. I prefer to use these settings when importing:

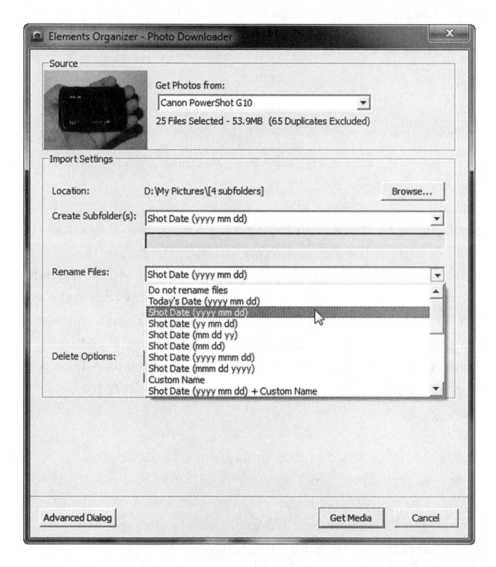

If for some reason your digital pictures get moved around on your hard drive, and you're trying to put them back in place, you do not want to face the situation where your computer software, or its operator (that's you…) thinks that two separate 1.jpg files are identical.

3 Steps to digitizing a photograph or document using the Flip-Pal mobile scanner

Many of the instructions below come directly from the Flip-Pal mobile scanner's PDF manual, but are included here (with permission) for your easy reference.

1. Power on the Flip-Pal mobile scanner.
2. Scan.
3. Copy digital images to your computer.

Step #1 – Power on the Flip-Pal mobile scanner.

Turn it on by sliding the spring-loaded power switch toward the rear, hold until the display lights up, then release. Set your resolution preferences. Here is what the LCD display shows:

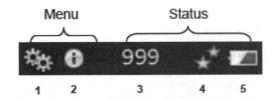

Menu	Status
1. Custom Settings: • Resolution • Power-Saver Timer **2. Quick Tips**: Reminders on how to use the scanner.	**3. Estimated Scans Remaining**: **4. Resolution Indicator**: • 1 yellow star: 300 DPI: fastest scan, smaller file • 2 yellow stars: 600 DPI: more detail, good for enlargements **5. Battery Life Indicator**

To access the Settings menu, press the UP ARROW from either the Home or Review Screen, then press the DOWN ARROW to get into the settings menu. You will see the following screen. Current settings are indicated with a green checkmark.

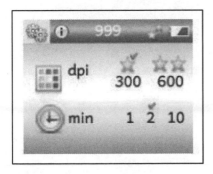

To set the resolution:

- Press UP ARROW to highlight the Settings icon. The current or factory settings will have a checkmark above them.
- Press DOWN ARROW to move into the Resolution (dpi) menu.
- Use RIGHT ARROW to highlight the desired resolution setting.
- Press OK to select.
- Press OK again to move back to the Home screen or the Review Screen, if there are images to review.

Step #2 – Scan

You can scan originals up to 4x6 inches.

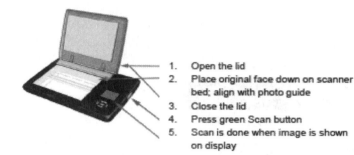

1. Open the lid
2. Place original face down on scanner bed; align with photo guide
3. Close the lid
4. Press green Scan button
5. Scan is done when image is shown on display

Or Flip and Scan. Flip scanning allows you to scan a photo in an album or frame, scan large originals for stitching together later on your computer, or scan small objects such as coins. See the Flip-Pal's manual for complete instructions and for information about using its built-in software to stitch images together. To flip and scan:

1. Remove lid: Pull up on small tabs at ends of the Photo Guide

2. Flip scanner over onto original
3. Align by looking through the viewing window
4. Press green Scan button

Step #3 – Copy digital images to your computer.

The Flip-Pal mobile scanner stores scans on the SD memory card the same way your digital camera does. When you are ready to use the digital images, transfer them to your computer using a card reader.

- To remove the SD card from the scanner, push it in gently. It will then spring out slightly, allowing you to slide it out. Note: it is recommended that you power off the scanner before removing the SD card.

Two Steps to Transferring a Photograph from your Digital Camera to Your Computer

1. Connect your camera or card reader to your computer.
2. Import pictures to your hard drive.

Step #1 – Connect your camera or card reader to your computer

Once you have snapped a bunch of pictures with your digital camera, to move them from your camera to your computer is a matter of connecting the two together. Your camera probably came with a USB cable. Connect one end into the camera and the other into an open USB port on your computer and turn your camera on.

The problem with this method is that I often forget to turn my camera back off when I am done importing which completely drains the battery. The solution is to use a USB card reader like the one shown below. The reader plugs into the USB port of your computer, and then the SD card plugs into it.

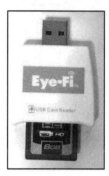

Or, computers, especially laptops, now come with the card reader built in so you may not need a cable or an external card reader.

Step #2 – Import pictures to your hard drive

Once connected, your computer may display the Windows Auto Play dialog. If you are using something other than Photoshop Elements, select the "Copy pictures to a folder on my computer" option and follow the prompts. You will need to manually browse to the location where you want to save the pictures. If you are using Photoshop Elements, click the Organize and Edit button.

If the Windows Auto Play dialog does not appear, open Photoshop Elements and go to File > Get Photos and Videos > From Camera or Card Reader.

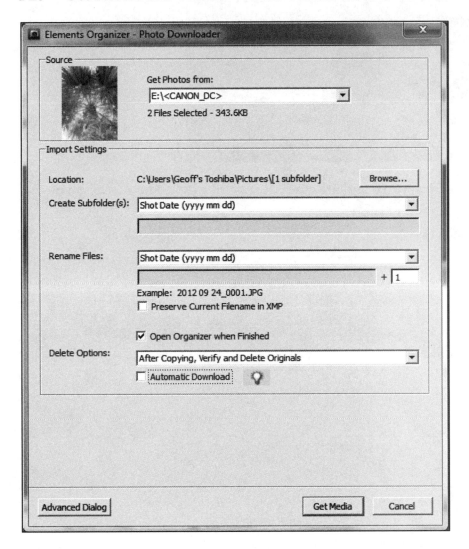

On the Photo Downloader dialog, your camera should be selected in the "Get Photos from:" section. Next, make sure that the "Location" is set to where you want to save the pictures. Next, within that folder, because the "Create Subfolder" choice shows the syntax of yyyy mm dd, it will automatically create folders based on the date that the pictures were taken. Finally, I prefer that the pictures are renamed to their shot date by choosing that option in the "Rename Files" section. Notice the example of "2012 09 24_0001.JPG" – this is how the file name will be saved when imported.

The last dialog you will see will be:

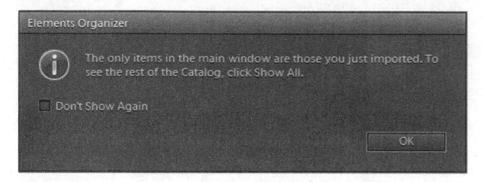

Your pictures have now been imported and are ready for your keyword tags (which you will learn about in the Organization chapter).

Before Editing the Picture

This newly-created digital image now becomes your original – I like to refer to it as the negative. Remember the old 35mm negatives? You would never intentionally (even if you could) try to alter the negative to make it better, would you? If you did, you could never get back to the original if you later wanted to. For example, you have a negative of a family picture – Mom, Dad, and the kids. You want to crop Mom's head so you can create a portrait of just her. Would you alter the negative to make this happen? Probably not. Your solution would be to develop that negative into a photograph, and then cut out her picture. You might even purchase five copies of the photograph to cut out each member of the family so they each have their own portrait.

The same principle is true when working with your original digital image. Before making any changes to it, like cropping, adjusting the exposure, fixing scratches, etc., first make a copy of the digital image. Previously you learned how to come up with a good file name. Let's use this file name:

   Brown, David and Clara.tif

I may want to make some changes to this "original digital negative" (the newly-digitized image), but before I do, I need to make a copy of it. There are a couple of ways of doing this. The safest way is to

1. Browse to the folder on your media (probably your hard drive) and locate the picture.
2. Then, right-click on it, and click copy.
3. Then, right-click on any open white space within the folder and select paste.

A copy of the original has now been created with a file name of:

   Brown, David and Clara – Copy.tif

An even easier method is found within the File menu of Photoshop Elements. Go to File > Duplicate. An exact copy of the picture will be created and the word copy is appended:

   Brown, David and Clara copy.tif

Now when you click Save, any changes are saved to the copy.

Now you can edit, crop, clone, repair, and touch up the copy any way that you want. The original will never be altered.

Auto-Editing Techniques

Most of your digital images are probably just fine, but when you come across one that needs a little help, Photoshop Elements, Picasa, or others are there to assist. The great thing is that software has come so far over the years that in many cases it can detect the problems and fix them for you.

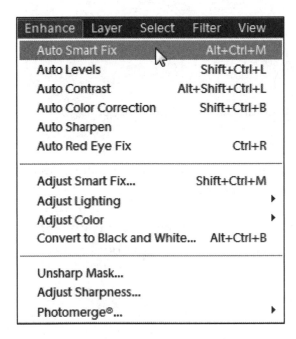

Photoshop Elements techniques

Before trying to fix the lighting, contrast, or color balance on your own, see if Photoshop Elements can do it for you. With a *copy* of your original file open (File > Open in the Photoshop Elements editor), click on the Enhance menu in the upper left and select the first option, Auto Smart Fix. If you shout for joy and are amazed at the change, I am guessing it did what you hoped. Save the changes to the file and you are done. If you do not like the result, choose the next auto command from the Enhance menu.

Here is how Photoshop Elements' help file describes each of the auto commands:

> *Auto Smart Fix* – Corrects overall color balance and improves shadow and highlight detail, if necessary.

> *Auto Levels* - Adjusts the overall contrast of an image and may affect its color. If your image needs more contrast, and it has a color cast, try this command. Auto Levels works by individually mapping the lightest and darkest pixels in each color channel to black and white.

Auto Contrast - Adjusts the overall contrast of an image without affecting its color. Use when your image needs more contrast, but the colors look right. Auto Contrast maps the lightest and darkest pixels in the image to white and black, which makes highlights appear lighter and shadows appear darker.

Auto Color Correction - Adjusts the contrast and color by identifying shadows, midtones, and highlights in the image, rather than in individual color channels. It neutralizes the midtones and sets the white and black points using a default set of values.

Auto Sharpen - Adjusts the sharpness of the image by clarifying the edges and adding detail that tonal adjustments may reduce.

Auto Red Eye Fix - Automatically detects and repairs red eye in an image.

If the Auto Smart Fix command does not work for you initially, experiment with each of the other commands until you are satisfied with the outcome. If you try a command and do not like it, just undo it by clicking Control-Z or going to Edit > Undo.

Another method of using the auto command controls is to initiate the process from within Photoshop Elements' Organizer. In the lower right, click on the Instant Fix button where you will find the same six auto commands.

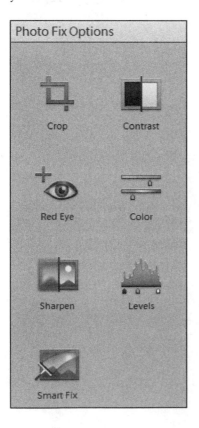

Initially one might think it could be dangerous to click on these buttons without first creating a copy of the image to work on. No need to worry – when one of these auto command buttons are clicked, Elements automatically creates a copy of the original and applies the editing changes to it. The edited image now appears "on top" of the original in what is called a version set. If you look closely, just to the right of the picture is an arrow. Clicking on it expands the version set so you are able to see both the original and the newly-created edited image. A terrific tool!

Picasa techniques

Before trying to fix the lighting, contrast, or color balance on your own, see if Picasa can do it for you. But first, a special note about editing a picture with Picasa. From its help file we learn that "when using editing tools in Picasa, your original files are never touched. The photo edits you make are only viewable in Picasa until you decide to save your changes. Even then, Picasa creates a new version of the photo with your edits applied, leaving the original file totally preserved." This is great news – Picasa, too, understands the importance of preserving your original so you can make edits knowing that your original is safe.

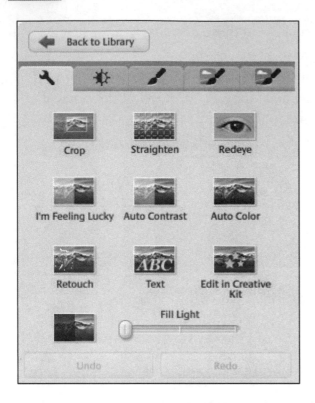

With your picture open (double-click on the photo in Picasa), click on the Commonly Needed Fixes button in the upper left (has a picture of a wrench). Click on the "I'm Feeling Lucky" button. If you shout for joy and are amazed at the change, I'm guessing it did what you hoped. Save the changes to the file and you are done. If you do not like the result, click the "Undo I'm Feeling Lucky" button and choose the next auto command.

Here is how Picasa's help file describes each of the auto commands:

I'm Feeling Lucky - This is the one-click fix. Picasa adjusts your photo's color and contrast to produce the ideal photo. You'll see a change only if your photo isn't already color balanced.

Auto Contrast - Automatically set the brightness and contrast to optimal levels, while preserving a photo's color values. A great way to fix a flat photo.

Auto Color - Automatically removes color cast and restore the color balance, while preserving contrast and brightness values.

Redeye - The Redeye tool will automatically correct red eyes that it detects in your photos for any photo file type that Picasa supports.

After you are happy with your editing changes, save the new file by going to File > Save. A confirmation message will appear, "Save Changes to Disk? A backup of this file will be made." Click Save. You now have an edited version of the image and the original. The new, edited file will remain in the same directory, but Picasa has moved the original. Locating this original is a little tricky though unless you know where to click and which option to select. Thankfully, you are reading this book! Right-click on the picture and click Locate > Original on Disk. The original was actually moved to a new hidden folder within the original folder. Using this Locate tool is the easiest way of locating the original. If you are unhappy with the revised image, and want to revert back to the original, thus deleting the newly-created/modified image, right-click on the picture, select Revert, and click the Revert button.

Editing: Advanced Tips and Techniques

About twelve years ago while trying to locate living descendants of David Brown I found a genealogy gold mine – in Alaska! I located one of David's granddaughters, an 80-year-old mother of two, who had the original family bible, Civil War papers of her grandfather, and dozens of old pictures. Since her children were not interested, she asked me what she should do with everything. Of course I knew exactly what she should do. Her 150-year-old collection of family artifacts is now in my safe-keeping. I have digitized everything in case anything happen to it.

While the photographs are precious, the effects of time have cracked and faded many.

Notice the poor lighting, a small rip, and a few scratches in this original. While there is nothing I will do to the original photograph to fix these problems, they can be corrected digitally and it is not that difficult if you know which tools to use. Most photo editing programs offer a variety of tools, to write about everyone would be beyond the scope of this book. While these step-by-step instructions pertain to Photoshop Elements, look for similar features in your favorite program.

The first step to restoring this photograph is to use the techniques described in the Basic Editing Techniques section. After making a copy of the original, I used the **Selection Brush Tool** to select just the photograph part. It is really small here, but try to notice the dotted selection lines. This tells Photoshop Elements which part of the picture I want it to work on.

Next, use the Auto Commands found in the Enhance menu. The Auto Smart Fix command did not make much of a difference, but the next command in the list did. Selecting the Auto Levels command gave this result:

Next, let's zoom in on the tear just above his head:

Digitally, the reason for the appearance of the tear is because the brown pixels in the area are not consistent with the lighter pixels that make up the rest of the background. If we could somehow "clone" the good pixels (the lighter ones) and replace the bad pixels (the brown ones), then it would appear as if there were no tear.

Clone

This is where the **Clone** tool comes in. It will become your best digital imaging friend. Most photo editing software programs have a Clone tool, although Picasa is not among them. Picasa does have a Retouch tool which can work in certain, smaller situations. With the Clone tool, you tell the software to replace certain groups of pixels with another group of pixels. Here is how it works in Photoshop Elements:

1. Zoom in on the area to get a closer look.

2. Click on the Clone button (found in the Enhance section of the Expert mode). I adjusted the brush size to about 10 pixels (found in the lower left).

3. Set the source point. While holding down the ALT button on your keyboard, click on the part of the picture that has the good pixels that you want to duplicate to replace the bad pixels.

4. Paint over the bad pixels. Click and hold the left mouse button, and drag the cursor over the bad pixels. This will take a little practice. In the end, the rip will no longer be noticeable.

The Clone tool can be used to fix scratches, tears, and even to add or remove objects from a photo. Every year our family goes out to the Arizona desert to take the annual family portrait. With young children it has always been difficult to get just the right picture, and so using the camera's timer button we take a few dozen. In 2007 we climbed to the top of this hill and finally got a picture we were happy with.

Back home, just before I ordered the enlargement (from www.ritzpics.com) that would hang on our wall, my wife noticed an unwanted object in the picture. She did not like how her leg was sticking out. She suggested that we go back to the desert and retake the picture. I knew that was not an option because my two oldest boys had been running around at the top, fell down, and scraped up their knees pretty badly. So I opened Photoshop Elements, pulled out the clone tool, and a couple of minutes later I asked if this picture would work:

Some historians and geographers get upset with me when I show them this. Notice the new mountains in the background on the left? Using the clone tool, I set the source point by clicking on the mountains on the right. Then I started painting over my wife's leg. No more leg. No problem. But our descendants will have a problem locating the exact location of the picture.

Zooming in on the bottom of the picture is a piece of trash.

Using the Clone tool, I was able to replace the white shades of pixels with the brown ones:

And just for fun, my youngest son loves adding new objects to his pictures with the clone tool:

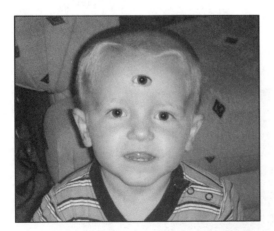

Hopefully you get the idea. Use Clone to repair digital images, remove unwanted objects, fill in missing elements, or even have a little fun with the grandkids. Once your picture is how you want it, print out a new one or upload it to a photo printing service to have it professionally printed.

Fixing little scratches and blemishes

For fixing minor scratches, small water spots, or dust marks, use the **Spot Healing Brush** tool. All you need to do is click on its icon in the toolbar, then draw over the scratch by holding the left mouse button down. When you let go of the button, the scratch will probably be gone. If you are not yet satisfied, paint over it again. It is an amazing tool. Picasa's equivilent to this is called the Retouch tool.

This tool came in handy recently when my sister sent me this email:

> "Any chance you would help me fix this picture of Austin? He has a little scrape on his nose that I want taken out of the picture and you are way better at photo shop than I am."

She was right about the scrape on his nose, although it looks more like someone threw a strawberry at it. And I guess she was right about the Photoshop part, except for the fact that I did not have to know a whole lot about Photoshop to easily fix the image. I just had to know about the availability of the Spot Healing Brush Tool and how to use it.

With her permission, here is a close-up of my nephew's nose:

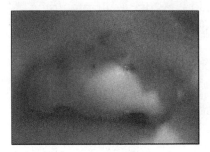

Here's how I fixed it.

1. Before making any edits to an original (especially if the original is in the JPG format), first make a copy of the original. I did this in Photoshop Elements by going to File > Duplicate. Now any changes I make will not harm the original.
2. After zooming in on the nose, I clicked on the Spot Healing Brush Tool and enlarged its brush size to about 35px.
3. Then I clicked and held the left mouse button down and highlighted the scraped area. When I let go of the button, the picture had pretty much fixed itself.
4. Save the new image at File > Save As.

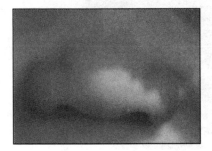

It took less than a minute from beginning to the end, but I guess sometimes you do need to know a little about what tools are available and how to use them.

Replace the background

Sometimes the background of the picture is so awful, that it is not worth the time to try and clean each individual blemish. Creating a new background and moving the person on top of it might be the easier and quicker method. (This is a little advanced, even for me...I found these instructions years ago, but do not remember where. They work great.)

1. Create the new background first. (Change to Expert Mode.) First, with the picture open, press Control-A to Select All. Then click Edit > Copy.
   a. Click File > New > Blank File. Click OK. Elements will now create a blank file that is the same size as your original picture.
   b. Press D to set your foreground and background colors to their defaults.
   c. Click Filter > Render > Clouds.
   d. Click Filter > Blur > Motion Blur, and select an Angle setting of 70 degrees, and set the distance to a large number, such as 800 pixels. Click OK.
   e. Click Filter > Blur > Gaussian Blur. Set the Radius to 30 pixels and click OK.
   f. Click Filter > Render > Lighting Effects. Choose Omni for the Light Type setting. Click OK. Now you have a custom background on which to place the person.
2. Now go back to your picture. Click on Image > Magic Extractor.
3. Use the Foreground Brush tool to paint on the person, or the part of the image that you want to keep.
4. Use the Background Brush tool to paint on the background. This tells Elements which part of the picture you want to remove.
5. Click on the Preview button and see how Elements did. If it removed too much of the person, click on the Add to Selection tool and paint the areas you want to add back to the picture.
6. Click OK. Select the Move tool, or just type V, and drag it to the other picture that you created with the background. (You might first have to click on the Photo Bin button in the lower left to see the other picture.)

Not a perfect job, and maybe not the best background color, but you get the idea:

How to "colorize" a black/white photo

I've been told that when my grandfather was my age we looked very similar. I wanted to see this for myself so I found an old photo of him. Our pictures looked nothing alike - his were black and white while mine were in full color!

Nothing breathes life into an old photo like adding color to it. Using Photoshop Elements (other software could probably do the job as well), it took about ten minutes to transfer history into colorful history.

Follow these steps to add color to a black and white photo:

1. Make sure you are in Expert Mode (click on the Expert tab at the top).
2. Make sure that the picture is in RGB mode. Look in the picture's title bar. If it says RGB, all is well. If it says Gray, click on Image > Mode > RGB Color.
3. Let's first "colorize" the skin. Click on the Create a New Layer icon at the top of the Layers palette. Rename the layer to "Skin".
4. Open another color photo that has a person in it. Click on the Color Picker tool and click once on the skin. The Foreground color is now the color of the skin. Close the color photo.
5. Click on the Skin layer to make sure it is the active layer. Type "B" or click on the Brush tool and select a smaller soft-edged brush.
6. In the Layers palette, change the layer's blend mode from Normal to Color. Set the layer's opacity to around 55% to reduce the intensity, or adjust it to look realistic.
7. Now start painting the skin. If the color appears to light to easily see the changes, change the layer's blend mode back to normal, paint all of the skin areas, and when you are done, change it back to color.
8. Let's add the hair color now. Click on the Create a New Layer icon, and rename the layer to "hair".
9. Open another color photo that has the color of hair that you want to use. Using the Eyedropper tool, set the Foreground color to the desired hair color.
10. Follow steps 4-6 again, but for the hair layer.
11. Repeat steps 2-6 for all areas of the photo that need color.

Stitching

Sometimes you run into the problem of the document being too large for the scanner. My scanner, which has an 8 ½" x 11.7" scanning surface is not quite large enough for the thousands of 8 ½" x 14" pension papers I copied at the National Archives.

Below are two separate images – the top 85% of the document, and the lower 85% of the document. It is the overlap of the image that enables the software to properly merge the two together.

To digitize and stitch/merge an oversized document, follow these steps:

1. Scan the top part of the document and save it.
2. Scan the bottom part of the document and save it with a different name.
3. In Photoshop Elements, click the Expert tab and then go to Enhance> Photomerge > Photomerge Panorama.
4. Click on the Browse button and select both files.
5. Click OK. If you get the question, "Would you like to automatically fill in the edges of your panorama, click Yes, and see how it looks.

The result is a beautifully-stitched document – the full 8 ½" x 14" document as one digital image.

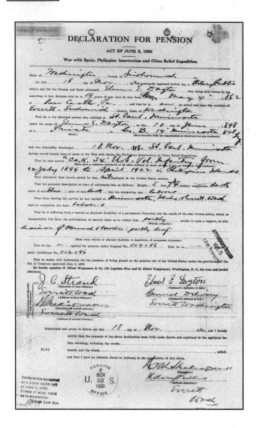

Another use for stitching is when you want to take a picture of a beautiful scene, but the scene is wider than the width of the picture your camera can take. With your camera, stand in the same place and take several shots, rotating a little each time to take separate pictures until you have photographed the entire scene. Make sure that with each picture you take that you overlap the previous picture by about one-third. This enables the photo editing software to effectively stitch everything together.

I found a beautiful two-story cemetery in Oslo, Norway. I stood atop and took seven pictures. With Photoshop Elements, I followed these steps to create the panorama:

1. In the Organizer, highlight each picture you wish to combine. Shortcut: click on the first picture, then Shift-Click on the last picture. This highlights all pictures in between.
2. Go to Edit > Photomerge > Photomerge Panorama.
3. Click the Add Open Files button, then click OK.
4. Crop the final, combined picture so the edges are filled in how you would like.
5. I like to then "flatten" the image (Layer > Flatten Image) so I can then Enhance the image (Enhance > Auto Smart Fix).
6. Save the new picture.

This new picture ended up being 88 inches wide – perfect to hang on my, uh, 88 inch wide extra wall.

How to selectively adjust dark areas of a picture

If only a part of the image is too dark, create an Adjustment Layer to fix it. Follow these steps:

1. In the Layers palette, click on the circle which is half black and half white. Click on Levels.
2. Drag the black Input Levels slider to the right until the dark area is lightened to your satisfaction. The rest of the image will be too light. We will fix this in the next step.
3. Select the Brush tool in the toolbar and choose a large, soft-edged brush (300 px should do).
4. Press the letter D to select the default foreground and background colors, then press X to set the Foreground color to black.
5. Finally, paint over the area of the picture that is too light. You might need to adjust the brush's opacity level (found at the top) to make sure the lighting is applied evenly.

Getting Organized

When I worked for a genealogy research company in Salt Lake City we had a goal to be able to file and retrieve any document in under a minute. Time was money. I have carried this goal into my personal digital filing system. If your digital collections number into the hundreds or even thousands, and you can locate any picture in under a minute, you know that you have a good digital filing system.

The organizational system I will describe below enables you to locate your digital pictures chronologically, geographically, by subject, by family, or even by face using facial recognition technology. Using these techniques you should be able to quickly locate what you are looking for.

After creating a digital image, either with your scanner or your digital camera, you have the choice of where to store that image. It can be stored on your hard drive, on a USB drive, a DVD drive, your camera's SD card, in a Dropbox folder, or even on a web server (the cloud). My recommendation is to use a combination, but always start in the same place – your hard drive. Keep in mind that any of these media can fail at any time, so make sure that you have a good backup strategy in place.

I store my digital images in two different locations on my hard drive.

> The *My Pictures* folder – for my personal photographs and scanned images

> C:\Genealogy Photos Pictures – for my digital genealogy documents

My Personal Photographs and Scanned Images

The *My Pictures* folder is where Windows stores your personal pictures by default. When importing pictures from your digital camera, almost always it directs you to save the pictures in the My Pictures folder. Within this folder it is a good idea to create subfolders to help you more easily manage your pictures. If all 17,861 of my personal digital images were in the same folder it would be more difficult to locate what I am searching for. Here's a snapshot of what the folder system looks like. Notice that each folder begins with the four digit year, followed by a hyphen, followed by the two digit month. With this syntax, the folders can easily be sorted by year.

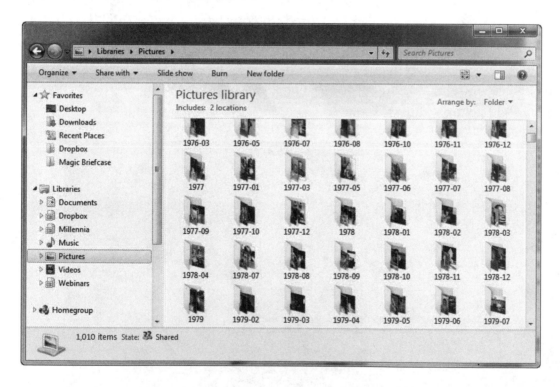

Inside the 1978-09 folder it looks like this:

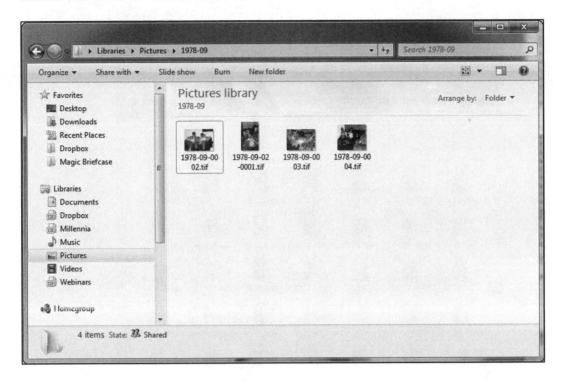

The file name of each picture in this folder uses this syntax: yyyy-mm-dddd-####
followed by the picture's file extension (.tif, .jpg, etc.). Because of how I have named these
files, it is not likely that I will ever have a duplicate of the file name on my hard drive.

I manually created these folders and files based on the approximate dates of the pictures.

Now that I use a digital camera, when the pictures are imported to my hard drive, the software creates the folder and file syntax (which I can manipulate if desired). Here's what the folders look like:

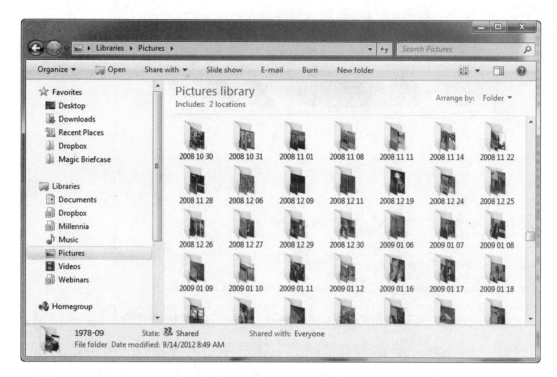

And here's what the files inside one of these folders look like:

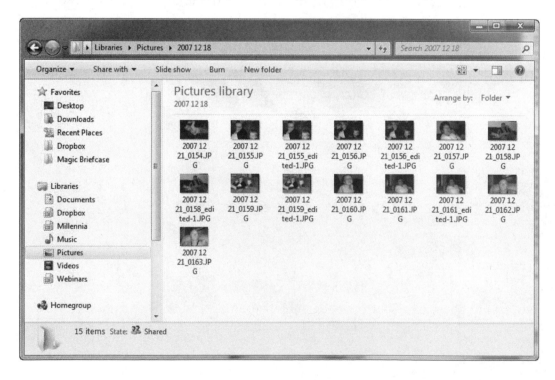

The files use the syntax of yyyy mm dd_#### followed by the picture's file extension. I think we take way more pictures today than we did before digital cameras.

To summarize – for my personal photographs and scanned images, I use the My Pictures folder with subfolders.

My Digital Genealogy Documents

One of my favorite repositories of genealogical information is the Family History Library in Salt Lake City. With their more than 2.4 million rolls of microfilm, over 1 million microfiche, and 3 billion pages of family history records, we are sure to find something about our ancestors. Combing through all these records without a catalog would be very difficult to locate your records. Their catalog, now known as the FamilySearch Catalog, lets you search for record collections in a number of ways, but more often than not we search for records in one of two ways.

First we locate records geographically. To see what their collections hold for Minneapolis, Minnesota, we would use the "Place-names" category and type in *Minneapolis*. The catalog reformats the location to display its geographic hierarchy in reverse order, showing us that Minneapolis is a sub-location of Hennepin (the county in this case), which is a sub-location of Minnesota (its state). Clicking on the Search button would present us with the register of their holdings for Minneapolis.

Second we locate records by surname. To see what their book collections hold for the surname of Brown we would use the "Last Names" category and type in *Brown*. Clicking on the Search button would present us with the register of their holdings for this surname.

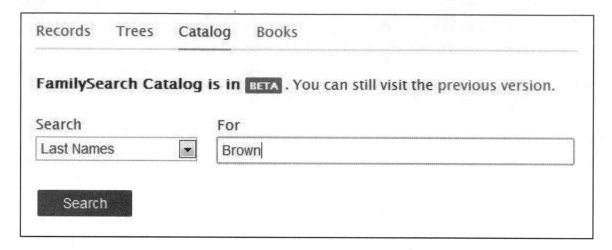

What does this have to do with digital images you say? I have set up my digital genealogy filing system to match the same organizational structure. Within my C:\Genealogy Photos Pictures folder, I have two sub-folders: Locations and Surnames.

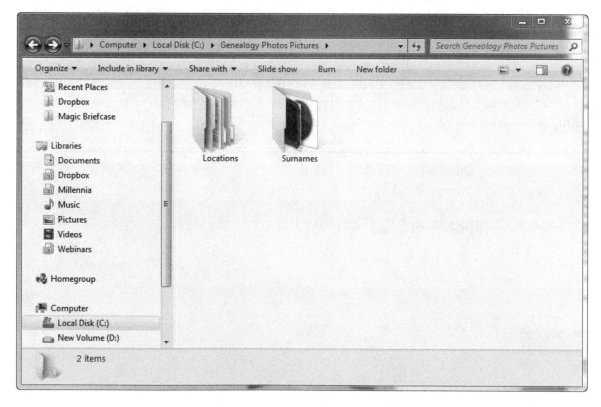

Within the Locations folder, I have created sub-folders for the countries for which I have digital images.

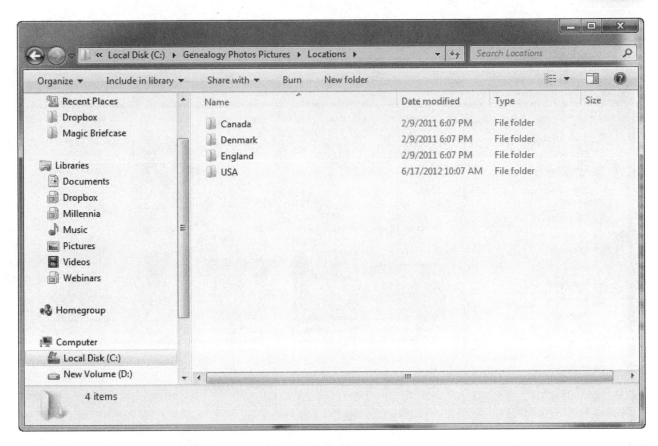

Within the countries, I have created sub-folders for each lower level of jurisdiction.

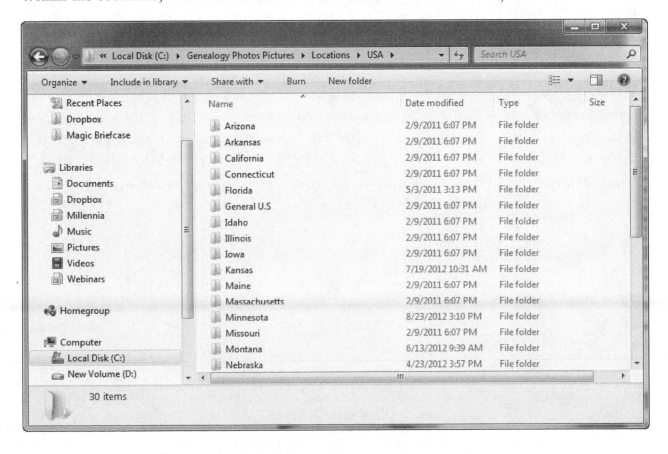

All the way down to the city/town/township level.

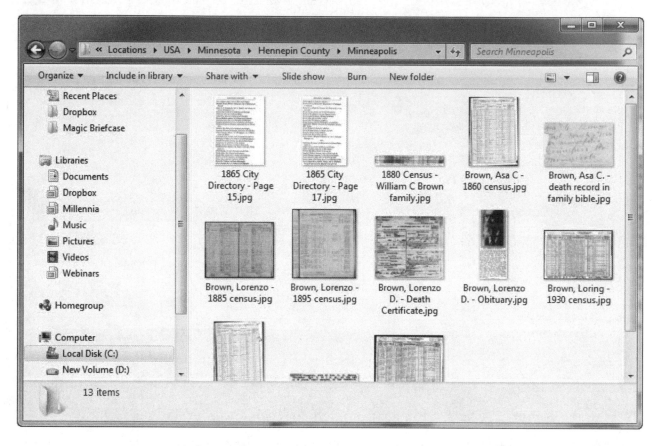

In most cases, if I were to try to locate these same documents in the FamilySearch catalog, they would be cataloged using the same directory structure as my digital filing system.

Within my Surnames folder, I store photographs, .pdfs of books relating to a surname, research reports I have written about that surname and more. To protect the privacy of my living relatives I have not included an image here, but within this folder, you can create as many sub-folders as you want. Again, in most cases, if I were to try to locate these same types of documents in the FamilySearch catalog, they would be catalogued using the same directory structure as my digital filing system.

Another Golden Rule

Once your digital files are stored on your hard drive:

- Do not move them to another location.
- Do not rename them.

At this point, you will probably link many of these digital images to your genealogy management software (like Legacy Family Tree! or others…). When you do, that software does not make another copy of the image to store it into its database. Doing so would not only duplicate the images, but because of the increased file size to its database, the database would become more and more unmanageable and more difficult to share with others. The genealogy software stores the *link* to the picture. It is able to create a small thumbnail of the picture to display to you, but keep in mind that it only stores the name and location of the digital file. If you change the file's name or move it to another folder or drive, the next time you open your genealogy software to view that picture, you will get some kind of "broken link" or "question mark" graphic. Good genealogy software provides the ability to relocate the picture, which works well if you have only moved the picture, but does not work well if you have either deleted or renamed the picture. It simply does not know what happened to it.

The same is true with your photo management software. For example, I somehow lost one of my early digital images. I either renamed it, removed it, but most likely it just flew away, because I would never claim fault for it....Let's just pretend that it was my fault. Photoshop Elements no longer knows where the picture is so it displays the following graphic instead.

Photoshop Elements does have a handy tool to try to reconnect these types of pictures (go to File > Reconnect > Missing File) but it is easier in the long run to follow these two golden rules. In my experience, Picasa, on the other hand, is able to locate pictures that have been renamed. However, if you move them to another location, make sure that Picasa is configured to also watch the other location for new files (go to Tools > Folder Manager for these settings).

Photo Organizing Software

Now that you have a little guidance with your folder and file system, are you able to use it alone to quickly locate anything in under a minute? Probably not. But since all of your photographs have now been digitized and saved on your hard drive, you have made a giant step in this direction. This is where a good photo management program comes in. Both Photoshop Elements and Picasa excel in organizing your digital media. Lifestory's *Heritage Collector Suite* software also deserves a look as it is organizational software developed by genealogists for genealogists, although it lacks photo editing tools.

Photoshop Elements

The first time you run Photoshop Elements it will ask you if you want it to scan your computer for any media. Click Yes and it will begin to happily crawl your hard drives for any media files. You are also given the choice as to which folders and drives to scan. Since I use the photo organizer software to manage only my personal media, I do not need it to scan my c:\Genealogy Photos Pictures folder. After making your selections, Elements will begin scanning. When it is complete, your *Catalog* will contain thumbnails of your media. The catalog contains information about each photo and media file, but it does not contain the actual file. Remember it creates a link to the original file. From Photoshop Elements' help file, "a catalog is like a database that contains links to your media files. These links inform Elements Organizer about the media file's location, file format, what keyword tags are attached to it, date the media file was taken, and so on. All of this information gives you flexibility in managing, identifying, and organizing media files." Although most people, myself included, prefer to have only a single catalog for all of their media, you can create more than one catalog. I might want to create a separate catalog for all of my wife's family pictures. Or a separate one for my genealogy documents, although I really just use my genealogy management software to manage those. If you want to create separate catalogs, go to File > Manage Catalogs.

In the future, when new pictures are added to your computer, they can be automatically added to the organizer, depending on your Watch Folders settings. At File > Watch Folders, I have it set to scan my My Pictures folders and its sub-folders, and to notify me when new pictures are added.

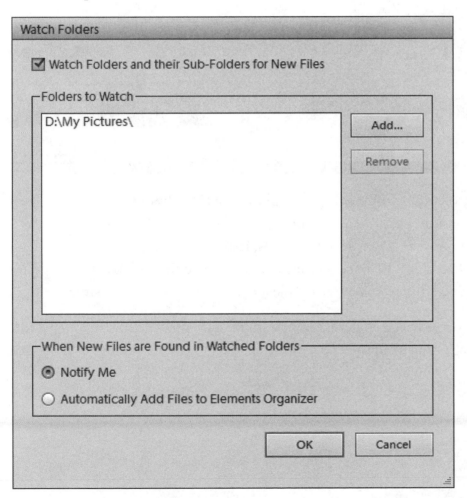

Regardless of where the digital files are stored in your folder structure, they all appear here in the same place:

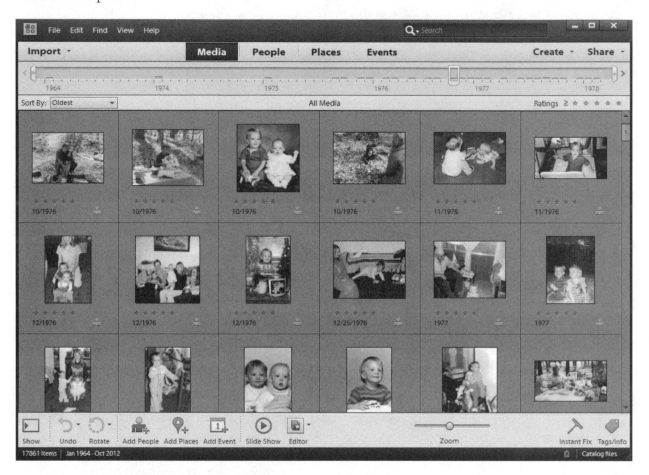

In the far lower left it displays the number of items in the catalog. Mine shows 17,861. Using the timeline filters found near the top, only 2,180 of those 17,861 are dated prior to my first digital camera in the year 2000. In other words, in the 25 years of my life prior to my first digital camera I had about 87 photographs per year. Since then I have averaged 1,289 per year. And aren't we happy when we find just *one* of our favorite ancestor?

By default, pictures are sorted chronologically. In the upper left you can choose to have the newest pictures at the beginning or at the end.

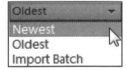

You may wish to change the size of the thumbnails so they are larger, but by so doing, you will see fewer at a time. Slide the bar to the left for more and smaller, or to the right for less but larger.

Finally, double-clicking on any thumbnail will enlarge it to fill the viewing area.

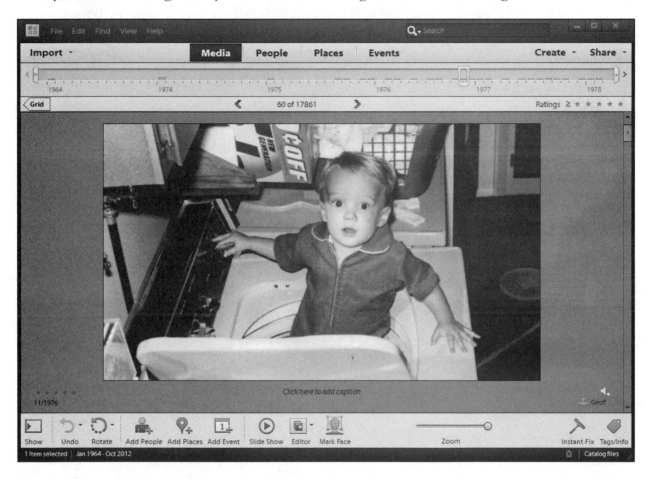

Picasa

The first time you run Picasa it will begin scanning your computer for any media files.
While it is not possible to disable the initial scan, you can use the Folder Manager to specify
the folders on your computer that Picasa should scan. Since I only use the photo organizer
software to manage my personal folders, I do not want it to scan and include the media in
my c:\Genealogy Photos Pictures directory. To control this, go to Tools > Folder Manager
and select the folders that you wish to include. Here you can tell Picasa to only scan that
folder (and its sub-folders) once, never, or keep a continual eye on any new activity.

Regardless of where the digital files are stored in your folder structure, they are organized here into the Picasa folder list.

By default, the folders are sorted chronologically. You can choose to sort the folder list by date, by recent changes, by size, or by name. If you click on the Reverse sort option, the folders with the oldest pictures will sort to the top.

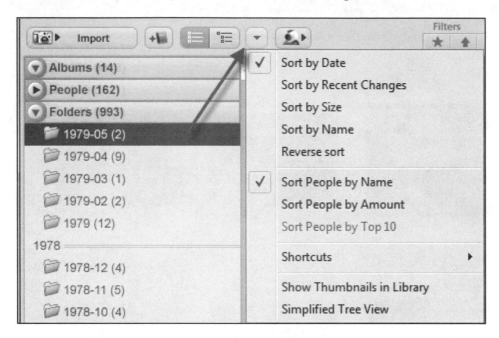

You may wish to change the size of the thumbnails so they are larger, but by so doing you will see fewer at a time. Slide the bar to the left for more and smaller, or to the right for less but larger.

Finally, double-clicking on any thumbnail will enlarge it to fill the viewing area.

Keyword tags, and facial recognition

Now that all of your pictures are in one place (…well…they are not really all in one place…the thumbnails of your pictures are all in one place…) are you now able to easily locate any picture in under a minute? Probably not yet. Although they are all sorted chronologically, you probably cannot remember what year that family vacation to Yellowstone was, or exactly when your child's first basketball game was. This is where keyword tags and facial recognition come in. Both Photoshop Elements and Picasa have these features and they work similarly. Elements uses the terms *keyword tags, people tags,* and *people recognition* while Picasa uses the terms *tags* and *name tags.*

Photoshop Elements' keyword tags

Keyword and people tags are personalized keywords, such as "Mom" or "Yellowstone" that you attach to your media. They enable you to easily organize and find the tagged files. From Elements' help file we learn that "when you use keyword tags, there's no need to manually organize your media files in subject-specific folders or rename files with content-specific names. Instead, you can simply attach one or more keyword tags to each media file. Then, you can retrieve the media files you want by selecting one or more keyword tags in the Keyword Tags panel. You can also find media files with specific keyword tags when you type a keyword in the Search textbox."

For example, you create a people tag called "Kaitlyn" and attach it to every media file (pictures, audio clips, videos) that features my daughter, Kaitlyn. Then, to instantly find all the media files of Kaitlyn that are stored on my computer, select the 'Kaitlyn' tag in the People Tags panel.

Let's take a look. If the right panel is collapsed, click the Tags/Info button in the lower right. If the People Tags section does not appear, go to View > Show People in Tag Panel.

By default, there are four categories: Nature, Color Photography and Other. I replaced these with Place and Events, and in the People Tags section, I added two sub-categories, Family and Friends:

Within the Family sub-category, I added more sub-categories:

Finally, within the "Rasmussen, Geoff" sub-category, I created keyword tags:

These tags are a little different from the Media, People, Places, and Event tabs at the top. These were introduced in the latest edition of Photoshop Elements. The Media tab shows *all* of your media. Clicking on the People tab will show you those people that you have tagged using the People Recognition tool. Places lets you assign places to your pictures using an online map, or, if your pictures already have GPS coordinates, they will automatically show in the correct locations. The events tab lets you assign certain events. If you used the keyword and people tags in previous editions of Photoshop Elements, like I have, they will appear in the Tags panel on the right.

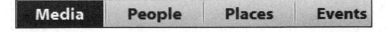

Next is the fun part. This is where you get to associate the picture with the keyword tag. All you need to do is drag and drop the keyword tags on top of the appropriate pictures. So for each of my wedding pictures, I would drag and drop *both* the "Geoff" people tag *and* the "Tanya" people tag on top of the pictures.

Each picture can have multiple tags linked to it. Therefore, if, in the future I want to easily locate all of my wedding photos, I might also create a keyword tag within the Events category called "our wedding" and drag/drop that tag on each of these pictures as well.

With hundreds or thousands of photos in your organizer the initial process of creating and linking the tags to the photos will take some time – probably a couple of weeks, maybe even a month. Be patient because it is so worth it!

Once the tag is linked to the picture, it is just a matter of clicking the arrow next to the keyword tag. Below I have clicked in the box next to my Grandma Rasmussen's keyword tag. Immediately the 17,861 photos are filtered to show just the 11 pictures I have of her.

When my son, Evan, asked to see if there were any pictures of him with his great-grandmother, I then clicked next to his people tag. With both keyword tags selected, the gallery was filtered to show just three pictures.

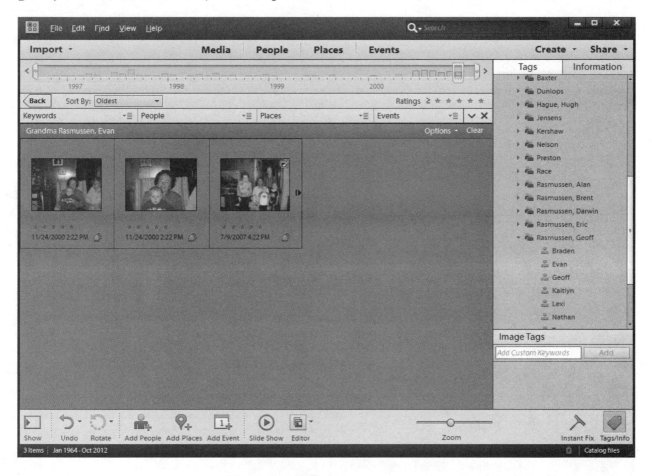

At the end of each year I choose one family photo to enlarge and hang on our wall. It is simple because as I import the pictures from my digital camera, I take a couple of extra minutes to drag the keyword tags on top of each picture. To locate the candidates, I simply click the arrows next to each member of my immediate family AND using the timeline bar at the top (or View > Set Date Range), I can filter the pictures even further to only include the pictures of that year. Looks like I've got 21 choices for the year 2012 so far:

It is possible that with the above example, even though I selected the keyword tags of everyone in my immediate family that other people appear. Other photos will still contain all six of us, but may also contain other cousins, grandparents, etc. As much as I love my extended family, I would rather they not be included in the family portrait for the wall. If, for example, my mother, Debbie, appears in some of the pictures (because her people tag is associated with every picture in which she is included), I can right-click on her people tag in the people section just above the gallery and select the option to "Exclude":

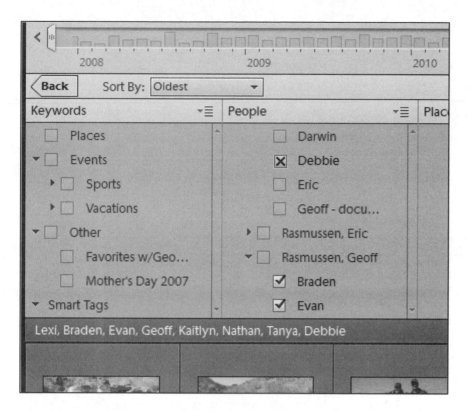

Do this for anyone else's people tags that may appear in your family pictures.

Next, because it took some effort to create the final filter (Geoff, Tanya, Evan, Nathan, Braden, Kaitlyn, but not Debbie…), it will save you time in the future by saving the Search Criteria. Just above the gallery, click on the Options button, then select "Save Search Criteria as Saved Search." In the Albums section (just above the Keyword Tags section) click on the green plus sign and select the third option down to "Save Search Criteria As Smart Album…"

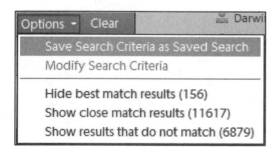

Then type the name of the Saved Search:

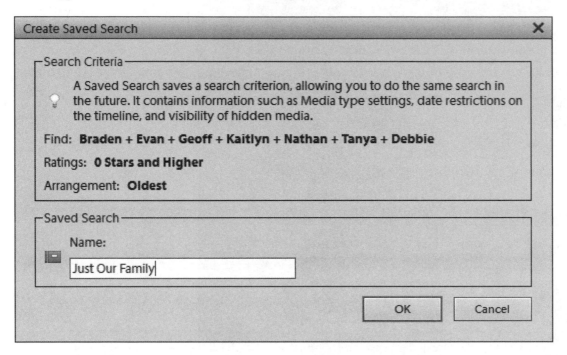

In the end you will have a new Saved Search. Now, anytime you want to filter your thousands of pictures to match the filter you created, you can just click on the Saved Searches option under the Search panel in the upper right.

Are you excited yet? Or should I ask, how excited are you now???

Photoshop Elements' People Recognition

Newer technology has given software the ability to use facial recognition techniques to analyze the photographs and automatically create people tags. This gives you a little less control over what gets tagged, can incorrectly identify people (like my daughter and brother who have similar facial features), and can exclude people when it is unable to find enough facial features to positively identify someone. For these reasons I do not particularly care for the feature, but it really is quite neat. If you want to explore it, here are the basics.

To get started, click on the Add People icon at the bottom.

Next, click on each picture and type in the person's name. This will create their people tag. After clicking Save, it will ask you about several more pictures. And then several more. The more you identify, the better its facial recognition features get. By the time you are done, most of the pictures in your catalog will be identified and tagged.

Picasa's tags

Like Photoshop Elements, Picasa lets you create tags to associate with your pictures. By creating and applying tags you can quickly search and locate your photos. To add a tag to a photo follow these steps:

1. Select the photos to tag. You can only tag photos in one folder or album at a time.
2. In the lower right, click on the Tag button to open the Tags panel. Existing tags and tag counts for the current folder or album will be listed.
3. There are two ways to add tags:
   a. Type the tag manually: use the text box to enter the tag and click the Add Tag button.
   b. Use your Quick Tags: By presetting tags that you frequently use, you can add them with the click on a button. Manage your Quick Tags by clicking the Configure Quick Tags icon in the Tags tab.

Chapter 9 ◇ **Getting Organized**   101

Once your photos are tagged, you can use the search box in the upper right-hand corner to quickly find pictures that you have tagged:

Picasa's name tags

If you would prefer not to manually tag every picture, Picasa's Name Tag feature is one of the areas where the program really shines. Just like Photoshop Elements, it will not do a perfect job. Nor can it really replace your efforts in identifying each and every photo, but it is just really neat!

Click on the People group in the left panel and off Picasa goes. When you click on the "Unnamed " name tag, it will show you thumbnails of unidentified faces it has collected. Below it found 86 groups (each group can have dozens or hundreds of faces that Picasa has detected as belonging to the same person – you can click on the Expand Groups button to see everyone in the group) and 6,330 faces.

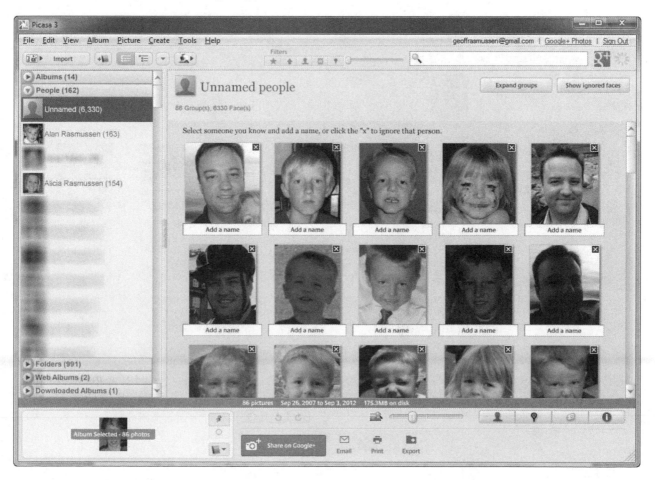

When you type in that person's name, everyone in that group is now tagged with that Name Tag. For instance, for the top left picture above I typed in my name, which brought the total unnamed faces down to 6,284. There must have been 46 pictures in that particular group where my face was identified in the photo. Now, because I identified that group as belonging to me, Picasa took another look at other unidentified photos with faces and would potentially suggest other pictures with my facial features in it.

The first time I did this I was stunned. I began by identifying a face of my mother, which I labeled as Debbie. It then took another look at the remaining unnamed faces and gave me another group of suggestions. In this next group were pictures of my mother when she was about twenty years younger. So I agreed with Picasa's suggestion by selecting her name, and thus associating this next group with her. It then found a bunch more pictures of her, this time when she was even younger. I do not know how it does it, but it must look for similar facial features such as the eyes, nose, glasses, and more to positively connect the same person over the years.

When you are finished identifying all the faces it presents to you, just click on that person's name in the People group, and immediately every picture where they are included appears.

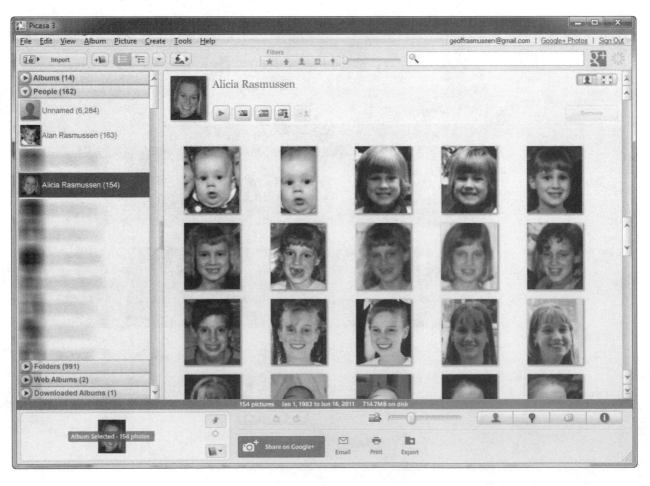

Double-clicking on any of the faces will open the full picture:

Compatibility of tags

So you have spent a lot of time tagging your pictures and identifying faces. You will now be able to find the pictures you are seeking much faster. What used to take an entire day or longer to find just the right picture now takes seconds – or faster! Years later you may decide to switch to a different photo management program. What happens to all the keyword tags and name tags? While these tags are proprietary to Photoshop Elements and Picasa, meaning other programs cannot use them, if you take one extra step, the keywords will forever be associated with the digital picture – even if you share it with someone else.

In Photoshop Elements go to "File > Save Metadata to Files." The keyword tags that you have created and properties information will then be added to the photo's *metadata*. Metadata contains information about the photo such as the date and time the photo was digitized, the shutter speed, the specific camera model and much more. Metadata can be viewed in the Properties panel:

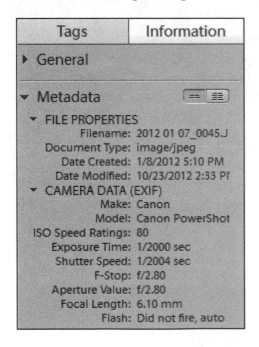

After writing the keyword tags to the photos' metadata, you should be able to use any other program's search features to search for the same keywords.

In Picasa go to Tools > Options > Name tags tab and make sure there is a checkmark next to "Store name tags in photo." This needs to be turned on at the beginning of your name tagging process because Picasa cannot go back and add this to photos you have already tagged.

Sharing

Sharing our digital photo collections has never come with so many choices, yet if you understand some basics it can a simple and fun process. There are five main ways of sharing digital photos:

- Printing and mailing
- Emailing
- Dropbox
- CDs and DVDs
- Website via the cloud

Printing and mailing

With a good color printer, the right kind of photo paper, a stamp and an envelope, you can send any of your digital pictures to your family. First we will look at how Photoshop Elements and Picasa can help you print, and then we will look at some alternatives.

In **Photoshop Elements' Organizer** click on the picture you want to print then go to File > Print. On the right are the five printing options.

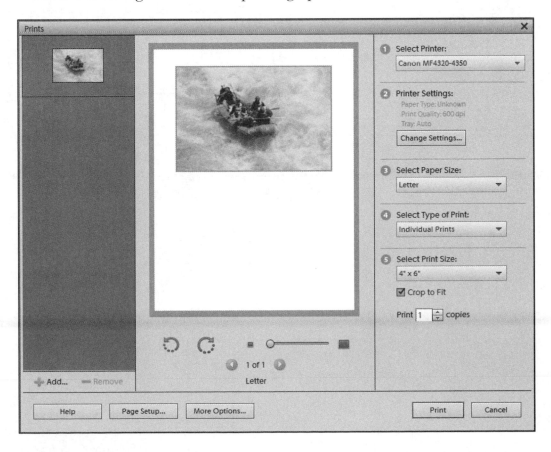

If you are printing a photograph, make sure to click the Change Settings button in step 2, then click on Advanced Settings. This will open the printer properties dialog, which will look a little different depending on your printer driver. Look for the setting to indicate to your printer that you will be printing photos. It will make some slight adjustments to optimize the printer for a photo print.

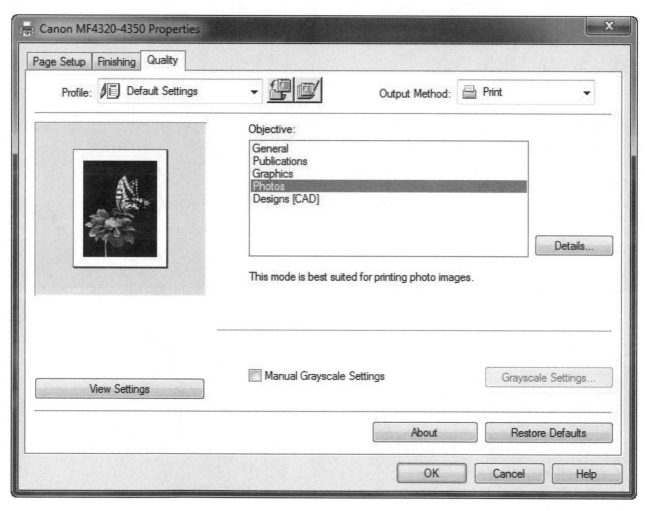

Back in the Organizer, if you want to print multiple pictures, select each by first pressing and holding the Control button on your keyword, then clicking on each photo. This Control-Click tool is a standard Windows function that enables you to highlight multiple files. When each photo has been selected, go back to File > Print and look at the different options in step 4. Here I selected four pictures, and selected the Picture Package option which provided several layout choices in Step 5. Play around with the choices until you find something you are happy with.

Picasa provides similar choices. Go to File > Print and pick your layout. Click on the Printer button to locate the printer driver's additional photo options.

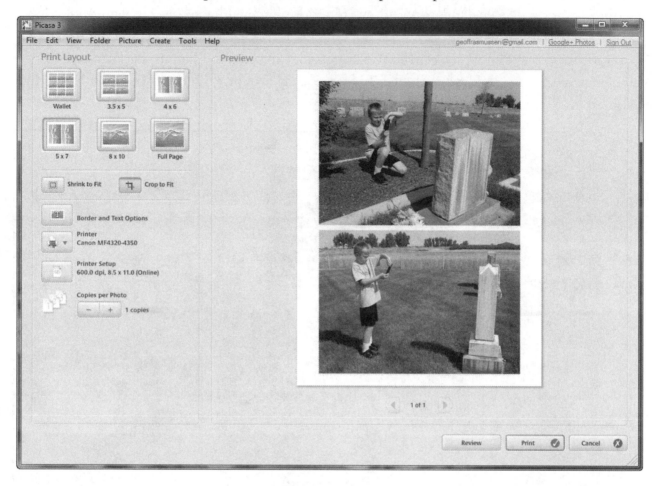

I no longer use the printer/photo paper/envelope/stamp method. Although my color laser printer did a fantastic job, I finally decided to give it away. The ink and photo paper just became too expensive to operate. My kids who enjoyed printing anything and everything in color may have had something to do with that decision though.

Now I use online photo printing services almost exclusively. These services all generally work the same. After creating an account and signing in, you upload the pictures you want to print, choose the size, the quantity, and a few other options, then tell them where you would like them to be shipped. I am a real sucker for these services because most provide many more alternatives to just printing the photo including:

- Collage posters
- Enlargements to 8x10, 11x14, 16x20, 20x30 and more
- Canvas prints
- Greeting cards
- Stationery
- Mugs
- iPhone cases
- Plates
- Puzzles
- Mouse Pads
- Necklaces
- Playing cards
- Blankets
- And so much more

Using my genealogy management software I created a five-generation picture tree, uploaded it to one of these sites, and purchased a photo placemat. Now, when my children are eating supper, they are also learning what their ancestors looked like, and at least five generations of their names. My kids also love the sheet of stickers with their portrait they get at Christmas.

A short list of online photo printing services include:

- Walmart.com
- Costco.com
- Shutterfly.com
- SmugMug.com
- Snapfish.com
- Samsclub.com
- Walgreens.com
- RitzPix.com

Emailing

Everyone uses email, right? Since the very first email I sent on August 28, 1998, I have sent hundreds, maybe thousands of digital pictures to family and friends via email. Think of how many stamps I did not have to pay for.

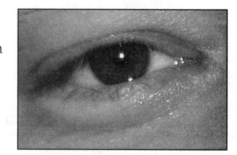

Emailing a digital picture can be simple but there are a few problems to overcome. Have you ever received a picture in an email from someone where you are only able to see the left eyeball? Or a picture so small that you can barely make out who is in it? The problem can be easily corrected by resizing a copy of the original photo before sending the email.

In **Photoshop Elements** open a picture in the editor and go to Image > Resize > Image size. Adjust either the width or the height in the Pixel Dimensions section. As you do, notice that just to the right of the *Pixel Dimensions* heading, the new file size will appear. I usually try to keep the new file size to about 1M:

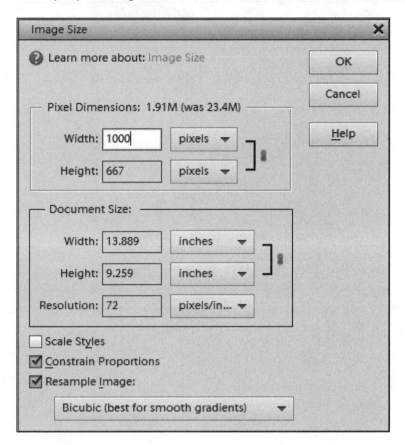

After clicking OK, go to File > Save As and give the newly-resized picture a different name (just add "-resized" to the end of the original file name). Then you can attach the picture to an email.

In **Picasa**, with the desired picture displayed, go to File > Export Picture to Folder and adjust the pixels to 800 or so. You can also adjust the image quality. The result will be an image ready to attach to an email.

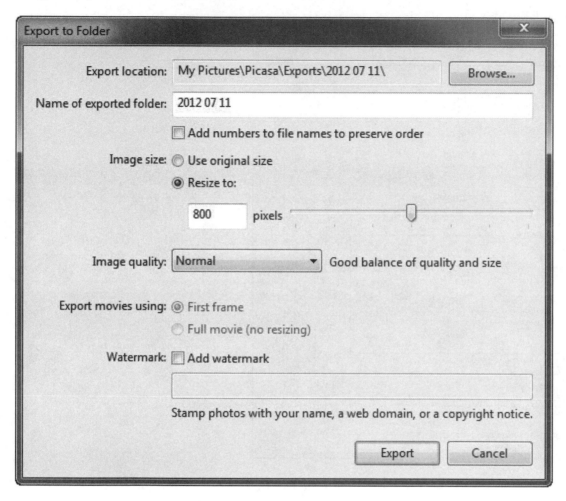

Another resizing tool called *Image Resizer for Windows* is found at http://imageresizer.codeplex.com/. It is independent of any photo editing software and makes it easy to resize your digital images. When installed, it adds an option to your right-click menus. In other words, when you are browsing your pictures in the Windows Explorer (sometimes referred to as My Computer), right-click on the picture that you want to resize.

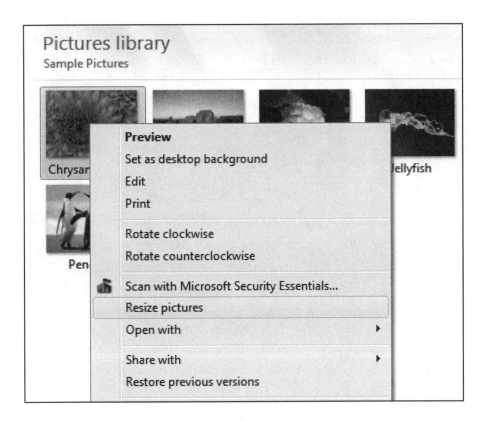

Then choose from one of the resizing options:

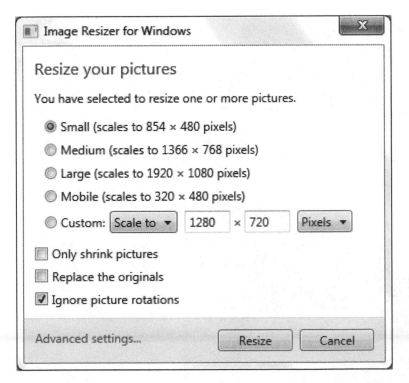

The result will be a brand new digital image with a slightly-modified name. It should be small enough to email now.

Once the picture has been resized, use your email software's attachment feature to browse for and attach the picture. You may need to consult its help section to learn how to do this, but generally, look for an "Insert File" or "Add Attachment" button, then locate the digital image, then send the email.

Email feature of your photo editing software

Above we discussed how to manually resize and attach a picture to an email. Photoshop Elements, Picasa, and others make it even easier with their built-in email features.

In **Photoshop Elements**, click on the picture you want to email, click on the Share button in the upper right, and choose either Email Attachments or Photo Mail. After making your resizing and quality choices, select the recipient of the email. You may have to first add them to your Contact Book. In the end, Photoshop Elements will send the email for you. Go to Edit > Preferences > Sharing to setup which email address you wish to use.

Selecting the Photo Mail option will embed your photo inside email stationary. You are able to choose the size, the email message, and include the caption. Makes for a fun and easy way to share your memories.

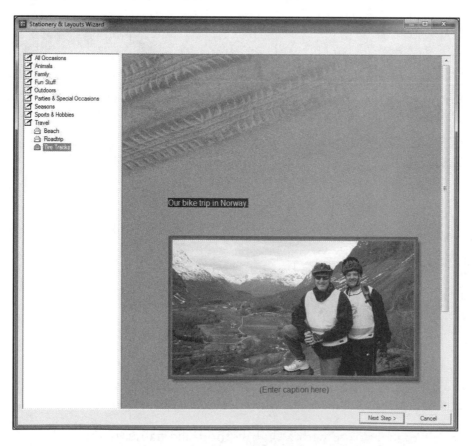

In **Picasa**, go to File > E-Mail, enter the recipient, the subject, and the message and click Send. Simple!

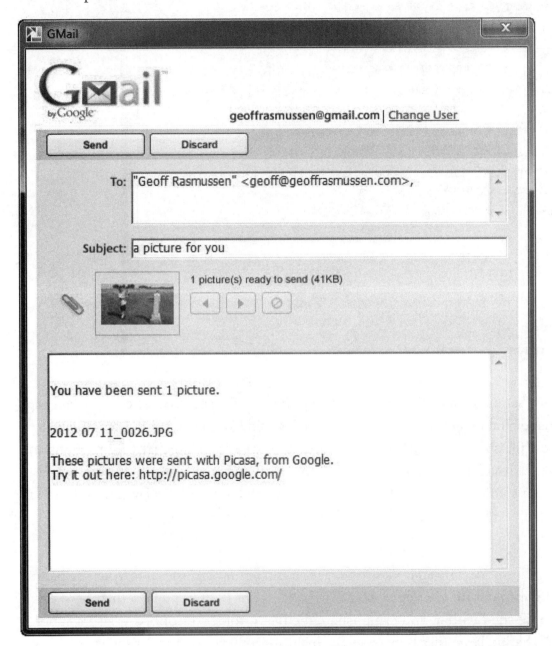

At Tools > Options > E-Mail tab you can select to use your Microsoft Outlook account or your Google account. If you use different email software it will need to be set up in your Default Programs (In Vista and Windows 7, go to Start > Default Programs). Once set up, it will appear in the E-Mail program portion of the E-Mail tab.

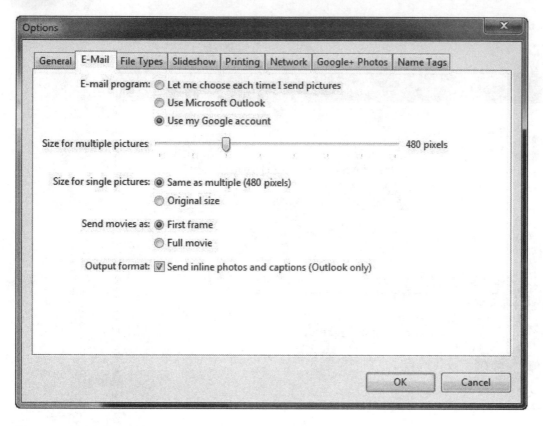

You can still send a large attachment

When someone sends me a digital picture, I sometimes prefer and request of them to send me the original digital image. If it is a picture that I would like to print out, I would like to have the largest file size and quality possible. If their picture is so large (email programs and Internet Service Providers may have limits on the size of an attachment) that it cannot be emailed, you can still use a service like Dropbox or youSENDit to send large files. Both are free to an extent, but the free versions will do the job. Visit www.dropbox.com or www.yousendit.com to learn more.

After installing Dropbox, through its software, you can grant permission to your recipient to access a file or folder on your computer. They then print it, or copy it to their hard drive. Once they are finished with it, you can unshare the file or folder. Dropbox is also a super simple way of sharing large files between your main computer and your laptop.

How to add a citation to a digital image
Ever seen a copy of an obituary without the newspaper's title or even the date? Newspaper clippings like this make it nearly impossible to correctly identify when and where it was published. Some researchers attempt to adequately identify a digital image by giving it a descriptive digital file name. In Elizabeth Shown

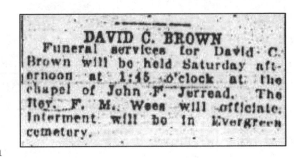

Mills' *Evidence Explained,* she comments that "aside from the insufficient identification of the source, another problem ensues. As the file is distributed electronically, others in the chain are likely to change the file label to suit their own filing system, thereby eliminating all clues to the source."

The solution is to add the citation to a copy of the original digital image.

To add a citation to the image follow these general steps:

1. In Photoshop Elements, if there is not enough white space at the bottom of the digital image, make space:
   a. Click on the Image menu > Resize > Canvas size. Change the anchor and width. Change the Canvas Extension color to white. Click OK.
2. Using the text tool type the citation.
3. Crop the image if there is any leftover white space.

It takes a couple of extra minutes to add the citation to a digital image, but the citation will always accompany the image when it is distributed with others.

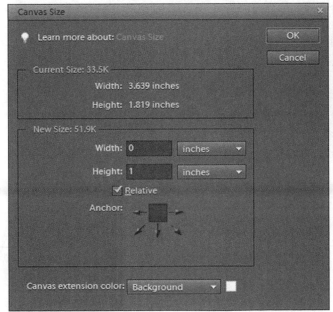

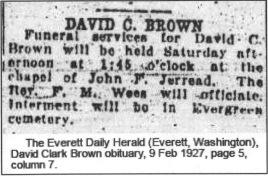

The Everett Daily Herald (Everett, Washington), David Clark Brown obituary, 9 Feb 1927, page 5, column 7.

CDs and DVDs

Not too long ago CDs and DVDs were the hottest, newest technology. With the emergence of USB drives and the cloud, it won't be too long before we classify CDs and DVDs in the same category as 5 ¼" floppies. (No research studies there, that's just my hunch.) Regardless, while they are still in the middle of their life cycles they are still valuable for sharing our digital media.

Copying our media to a CD or DVD is a good method of sharing – nearly everyone has the hardware to view their contents. It is the presentation and organization of how you share the media that makes the difference. Compare the two presentations below. The first is what the recipient sees when they insert CD #1. The second is what the recipient sees when they insert CD #2. Both CDs contain the same digital pictures and a copy of my genealogy database.

CD #1

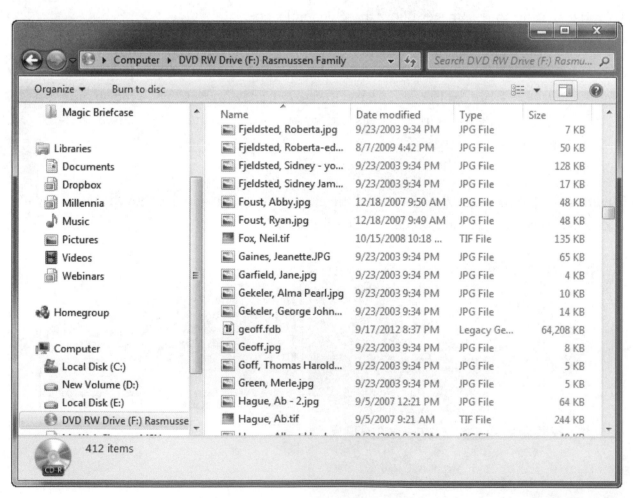

CD #2

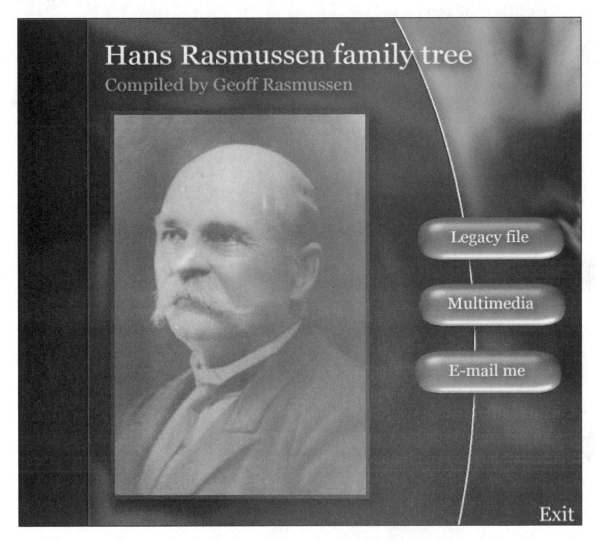

The family member who inserts CD #1 can double-click on each file to view it. The family member who inserts CD #2 can click on the Multimedia button and be presented with a narrated slide show of the same pictures, with faded transitions between each one, while listening to some nice background music that was included. I think you know my preference.

The Passage Express software created CD #2. From www.PassageExpress.com, it helps you create a nice menu with customizable buttons that is sure to impress.

Another photo management program, Heritage Collector Suite, from www.HeritageCollector.com, will create Gift CDs, with similar, yet more robust features than Passage Express. Both were developed with the genealogist in mind, so you will find many features unique to our industry.

Another method is found in **Photoshop Elements.** Click on the Create tab in the upper right, click on Slide Show, and select your preferences:

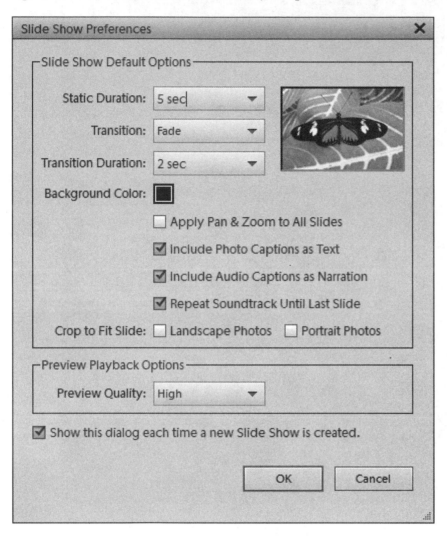

Click OK.

Then click on the Output button:

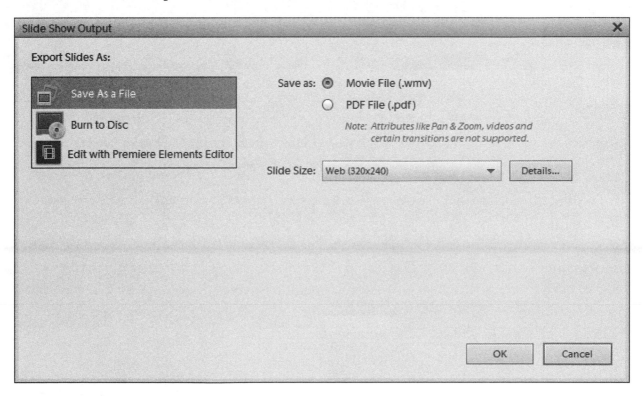

You now have a self-running video CD that can be played on your computer or TV using a DVD player.

Or, in **Picasa** select the pictures you want to include on the CD, then go to Create > Create a Gift CD.

Choose your selection and settings in step 1, name the CD in step 2, then click on burn disc. Unfortunately the gift CD can only be played on your computer. Separate authoring software is needed to create DVDs capable of being viewed in most DVD players.

Adobe Premiere Elements

My favorite movie authoring software is Adobe's Premiere Elements. It and Photoshop Elements are nicely integrated, meaning, using the photos in your Elements Organizer, you can create a more customizable slide show with a few clicks. Click on the Create tab, then choose either Instant Movie or DVD with menu. A message will appear saying that you need to have Premiere Elements installed (if you don't already), and it offers you a 30-day trial. Continuing on, it sets up your slide show but now you are in control of setting the transitions, the music, and even the opening screen and credits.

If you want to go this route, there are some settings and a recommended order of development steps I have come up with that work well:

1. Digitize your pictures
2. Pick software to create the DVD slide show: Adobe Premiere Elements, Passage Express, Heritage Collector Suite, Windows Live Movie Maker, or others
3. Using the software, import the pictures into your project
4. Organize your movie
5. Create transitions from one picture to the next
6. Add music
7. Add a title and credits
8. Set scene markers
9. Create the menus
10. Test the DVD
11. Burn the DVD
12. Create the packaging

And just like a real DVD movie, it will help you create a Scene selection menu:

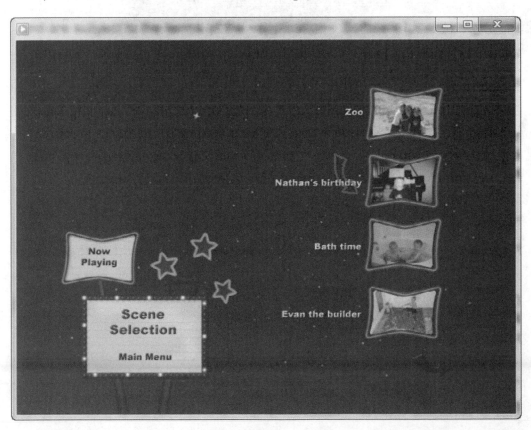

The credits:

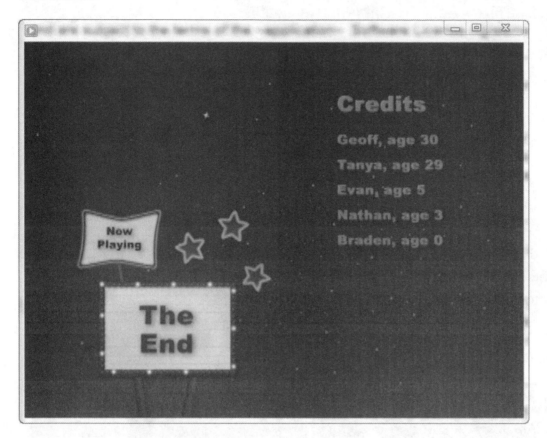

And even the DVD case insert:

Here are a few other video editing software choices:

- Corel VideoStudio Pro
- CyberLink PowerDirector
- Roxio Creator
- VideoPad
- MAGIX Movie Edit Pro
- Pinnacle Studio HD
- MoviePlus

Plenty of online services will help you convert your digital images into beautiful slide shows, complete with music, transitions, and credits too. They generally do not give you as much flexibility and creativity as you get from something like Premiere Elements, but they do a terrific job. Do an Internet search for "online video software." I only have experience with using Shutterfly's service which does an excellent job.

The Cloud

In my perfect digital images world, I would have access to my digital images from my home computer, my laptop, my smart phone, my tablet, and from any Internet-connected device in the world. I could view them, edit them, print them, or email them. My mother would also have access to *view* my pictures. My friends would have access to view certain pictures. And my genealogy colleagues would have permission to view selected genealogy digital files.

This perfect world is finally here. It is often referred to as the *cloud* or *cloud computing*. Wikipedia describes this term as "the use of computing resources (hardware and software) that are delivered as a service over a network (typically the Internet)." Sounds boring, doesn't it? What it means is that through the Internet, we can have access to our files from our computers or mobile devices, and we can grant others permission to access these files.

Living in the state of Arizona, our children are thousands of miles away from their grandparents in Oregon and Idaho. While we do not get to visit as often as we would like, we have bridged the gap a little through our digital pictures and the use of the cloud. To do this, I have configured my photo management software to upload my family pictures to a

private account on the Internet, and have granted my parents, my wife's parents, and other immediate relatives permission to view and print these pictures. The best part is that once the pictures are on my computer, it is an automated process to share them in this way – almost. I do have to intentionally tell my software which pictures I want to share. When new pictures are added my family is automatically notified of the updates.

4 Steps to Sharing via the Cloud

1. Digitize and organize the pictures on your computer with Photoshop Elements.
2. Using Picasa, create an album to be synchronized online.
3. Select which pictures to share.
4. Select who you will share with.

Here are the detailed step-by-step instructions with explanations.

Step 1. Using Photoshop Elements, I digitize and organize the pictures on my computer. You know how to do this by this point in the book.

Step 2. Next, in Picasa create an Album. The albums section is found at the top of the left side panel. Since each album can only hold 1,000 digital images, sometimes I create two albums for the year. Click on the blue Create a New Album button to create a new album.

Step 3 – If you have not signed up for Google+ (which is fine, I'm not yet a big fan…)

a) Click on the arrow next to the Share button and turn on the **Enable Sync** option. Any pictures in this album will now automatically be copied to an album in your Picasa Web Album. Access your Picasa Web Album by clicking on the **Web Albums** link in the upper right or just navigate to http://picasaweb.google.com. So far you have not added any pictures to the album.

b) In the Folders section of the left panel, click on a folder with pictures you want to include in the album. Select each picture in the album (remember Control-click selects multiple pictures; Control-A selects all pictures in the folder). Then, right-click on one of the pictures and select Add to Album, then select the Album name. These pictures are now included in your album which you have set up to synchronize with your Picasa Web Album. Again, you can now go online to see the new pictures being synchronized.

c) Customize your sync options by clicking on the arrow just to the right of the Share button. Here, you can adjust the privacy options and the picture sizes:
   a. Privacy options
      i. Public - Anyone on the web can view public albums. Public albums can be found on your public gallery, in web search results, on your Google profile, and in Google+.
      ii. Limited, anyone with the link - These albums are visible to anyone with the link. They're technically visible to anyone, but they include a unique authorization key in the web address; the key is a combination of letters and numbers that make the address difficult to guess.
      iii. Limited - Limited albums are visible to the people you specify, and those people must sign in to their Google Account to view your photos. Users without a Google Account will be prompted to create one. Google+ users: The people you share with have permission to reshare your album. Within Google+, they'll also be able to see who else you've shared with.
      iv. Only you - The highest level of privacy, these albums are visible only to you. Changing an album to 'Only you' will wipe everyone off the album's 'Shared with' list.
   b. Picture sizes
      i. 800 Max. Width - Uploads up to 800 pixels are free for all users of Picasa Web Albums. A good size for publishing images on blogs and webpages.

ii. 1024 Max. Width - Good for sharing online albums with friends and family.

iii. 1600 Max. Width - Recommended, great for prints, sharing online albums, or for use as a screensaver.

iv. 2048 Max. Width – Even better….

v.   Original Size Images - Uploads the image at the original image resolution (e.g. 4288 x 2848).

vi. Picasa's help file has some other important information: "Choosing your upload size affects the quality of the image you store online. Smaller upload sizes come at the cost of reduced image quality - especially important as the size at which you upload is the largest size at which your photo can be downloaded. Picasa gives you the option to preserve original image quality for smaller size uploads to Picasa Web Albums as well. This means that when Picasa creates and uploads a smaller sized JPG, it uses the quality settings of the original image to maximize image quality at the smaller resolution. Uploading images at sizes larger than 800 pixels count toward your free storage limits." To preserve the original image quality when you upload at a smaller size than the original photo:

1. Click Tools > Options (Windows) or Picasa > Preferences (Mac).

2. Click the Web Albums tab

3. Check the box next to 'JPEG Quality: Preserve original image quality.' This option is automatically enabled when uploading at 'Original Size.'

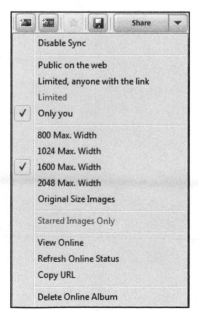

Step 3 - If you have signed up for Google+

If you have signed up for Google+ it will look a bit different. These features are pretty new to Google+ and frequently change, so at the time of this writing, here are the instructions:

a) In Picasa, select the photos you'd like to upload.

b) Click the **Share in Google+** button at the bottom of the Picasa window.

c) Select an album or click **New** to create a fresh one.

d) Choose an image size.

e) Share your photos with just the right people by adding your Google+ circles, individuals in Google+, or email addresses. Anyone you've tagged in the photos you share will be included in this box. You can remove them by clicking the X next to their name. Then add any other Google+ circles, individuals in Google+, or email addresses of friends and family to share with. You can also upload photos without sharing in Google+. Just make sure the + Add more people box is empty and click Upload.

f) Click Share.

g) A few things happen when you share your photos:

    a. The people tagged will be invited to view the tagged photo and the related album.

    b. People that use Google+ will see photos you share with them in their stream. People you share with who don't use Google+ will receive an email to view your photos in Google+.

    c. The people you share with have permission to share your album with others. If you'd like to disable the ability for others to reshare your album, you can lock the album in Google+.

Step 4 - Go to http://picasaweb.google.com to view your album online.
Click on the album to view its pictures:

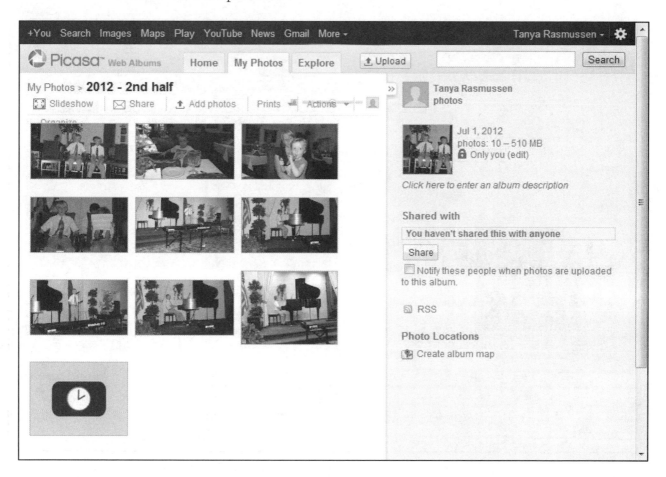

Then click on the Share button, type in the email addresses with whom you want to share the album, type a brief message, and click the Share via Email button.

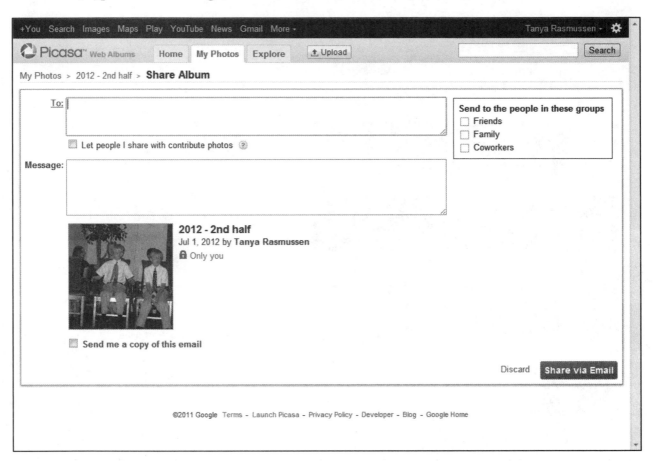

Finally, make sure there is a checkmark next to the Notify statement in the Share section to ensure that your contacts are notified whenever you add new pictures to the album.

I received this email this morning that my wife has added new pictures to one of her albums:

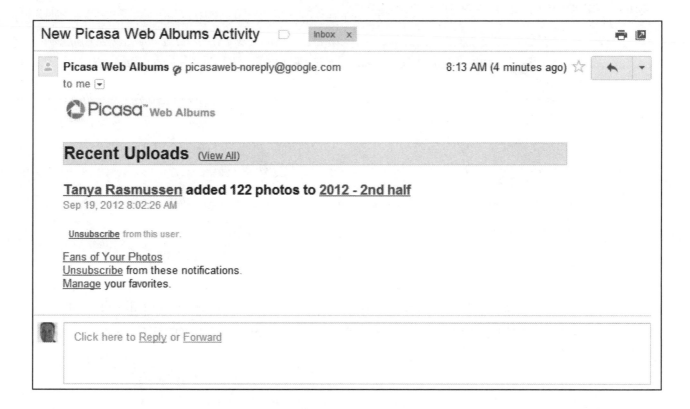

Picasa Web Albums offers 1GB of free storage for photos and videos. However, files under certain size limits (800 pixels wide or less) do not count towards this free storage limit. If you reach your storage limit when uploading from the Picasa desktop software, you will only be able upload at free storage sizes. Larger uploads will not be automatically resized to the free storage limit. But if you prefer to upload your images at a larger size for better quality (archival or print), you can buy more storage at any time at https://www.google.com/settings/storage/. The pricing is pretty reasonable.

Photoshop Elements has a similar cloud service, but because of its complexity and higher costs, I have stayed with Picasa Web Albums. Just this morning, I happened to check my email's Spam folder and saw this from Adobe:

As a valued Elements membership customer, we want to let you know that Elements membership will be changing in the next version of Adobe Photoshop Elements and Adobe Premiere Elements.

The next version of Elements will no longer support the in-product membership experience including syncing and storage. If you continue to use versions 7-10 of Photoshop Elements or Premiere Elements, the photos and videos in your catalog and albums will continue to be synced and stored. And rest assured they will also continue to be available online at www.photoshop.com.

We are working on some really exciting new technology that we think you will love and will share more with you in early 2013.

I have been very excited with the potential that Photoshop Elements' cloud technology shows, but until now it has not worked well enough (lots of bugs and very slow) and does not compete with Picasa Web Album's costs of storage space to merit my full use of it. So we'll see what the future brings. Stay tuned at www.photoshop.com for any updates.

Picasa Web Albums – anywhere

Now that your pictures are in the cloud, you can begin accessing them with your mobile devices. My android-based smartphone's screen is shown below. Using the web browser software, I navigated to http://picasaweb.google.com and my web albums appear (shown on left).

Tapping one of the albums brings up the display of all the pictures in the album (shown on right).

Tapping a picture displays it in this mode. I cannot count the number of times that having these pictures on my phone calmed my 2-year-old when she was sad. We could look at them in bed, at the store, anywhere! This same ability is available on my tablet as well.

About the only complaint I have had with this is when I am in an area where Internet access is not available for my phone. Without the Internet, I am unable to browse to http://picasaweb.google.com.

This is where a third-party app like **Perfect Tool for Picasa** comes in. Found in the Google Play store, it, too provides the ability to browse albums and look at individual pictures, but it also provides the ability to make the album available offline, meaning the pictures can be viewed even without the Internet – good for airplanes and basements where your phones Internet signal may not work.

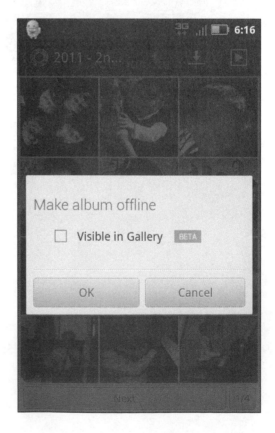

If you are like me and now carry your smart phone with you everywhere (I used to make fun of people who could not detach themselves from their phone) you always have access to your camera. With my current phone I have taken hundreds of pictures, but unless you transfer them from your phone to the cloud or your hard drive, you run the risk of losing them all. Fortunately smart phone software makes it simple to share the photos if you know where to look.

Here is a portion of my phone's gallery. It has pictures of the football game, my bowling high score (232!), and even a few home décor samples. Tapping on a picture brings up a share button, that leads to the "Select an action" screen where you have lots of sharing choices. Clicking the Picasa icon lets you add a caption and choose the album to which you wish to upload. Or tap the Facebook, Google+, or Dropbox icons to upload to any of these services.

Our discussion of cloud-based photo services would not be complete without at least a mention of some of the other online services. In addition to Photoshop.com and Picasa Web Albums, these also deserve consideration:

- Flickr
- Photobucket
- Shutterfly
- SmugMug
- Snapfish
- Facebook
- Google+
- SlickPic
- Many more…

Backup Strategies

I believe there are only two types of computer users in the world. One who has had their hard drive crash and one who will have their hard drive crash. If your hard drive is the only place you have stored your digital pictures, there is a good chance that you will lose everything someday. In fact, a couple of years back I received a frantic telephone call from a friend. He said, "my wife has done something to the computer…". Before he went any further I should have given him some marriage advice. He continued, "and now I can't get to any of my pictures." His hard drive failure was so severe that his digital pictures were unrecoverable. He lost five years of memories that day. But it did not have to happen.

In the **BDC** (before digital cameras) days we used to take our rolls of 24 or 36 to the photo store and have them developed. A few days later we returned home with hard copies of our photos. Today I wonder how many of us implement even a partial backup strategy like this? Of the 17,000+ digital photos in my photo organizer, I know I have not made physical prints of all of these – not even 10% of them.

There has never been a more important time to ensure that you have a good backup strategy for your computer's digital files. A good strategy includes the implementation of more than one of the backup suggestions below. I say more than one because one or more of these strategies could fail and you want at least one good backup.

- Backup to an external hard drive or another internal hard drive
- Backup using a cloud service
- Backup to CDs or DVDs
- Backup to a photo book

External hard drive or another internal hard drive

Inside your computer is a hard drive where all of your files are stored. Hard drives can fail for a number of reasons. Add to your backup strategy an external hard drive. In relation to the cost of what could be lost, they are very inexpensive. An external hard drive usually connects via a USB port on your computer and shows up in your "My Computer" area as a new drive with a new drive letter. Your hard drive is usually the C drive. Your CD/DVD drive is usually the D drive. When you plug in the external hard drive, it may be assigned the letter E or higher.

To backup your digital pictures, if they are stored in the My Pictures folder, navigate to this folder, right-click on it, and click Copy. Then navigate to the external hard drive's folder, right-click and click Paste. All of your pictures will then be copied to your external hard drive resulting in an exact backup of everything in that folder. To automate the process, you can use Windows' "Backup and Restore" utility found in the Control Panel or other software such as Acronis' True Image software or others. There are hundreds of them out there. Look for the ability to:

- Automate and schedule a backup
- Backup to the cloud
- Mobile file access
- Multiple restore points

After making a backup of every file, the backup software monitors your computer for any new or changed files, and the next time it makes a backup, it only backs up those files. This is called an incremental backup. I have mine scheduled to run at 11pm every evening. Obviously, the computer would have to be turned on for this to work. I do not remember the last time I actually turned mine off at night. I wonder if there is any correlation between that and my power bill? The nice thing about an external hard drive is that it is portable. When I go on vacation, I can take it with me just in case something happens to the house while I am away. Sometimes when I leave town I will store it in my fireproof safe. I have heard of people storing it in a safety deposit box at a bank.

I also have a second internal hard drive. These are a little more tricky to install, so I usually just ask the computer store to do it for me at the time of my computer purchase. Like an external hard drive, an internal hard drive not only provides more storage space, but could also be used solely as a backup drive. I have set up my backup software to also make an incremental backup to my internal hard drive each evening. If something happens to my external hard drive, I have another option.

Cloud services

If something happens to the room where your computer and external hard drive are located, both are at risk. This is where having a good backup at a remote location comes in handy. In addition to the external and additional internal hard drives, I also use an off-site backup service. This service will make incremental backups of your data, and using your Internet connection, will upload and store your data on a private web server to which only you have access. A couple of times I have had to request a copy of my data, not necessarily because I lost my entire hard drive, but because something happened to one of my documents. It was easier to request a copy of its latest backup then to try to recreate the document.

There are a number of off-site backup services, also known as cloud backup services, so check out their pricing and storage space. Some will offer free space to a certain point. I currently use BackBlaze (www.BackBlaze.com) because of their unlimited storage and reasonable monthly pricing, but have used others in the past. Here is a small list of options:

- BackBlaze.com
- Carbonite.com
- Mozy.com
- SugarSync.com
- CrashPlan.com

Do an Internet search for "backup services" or visit PCMAG.com or CNET.com for recent reviews.

CDs/DVDs

Since we have previously discussed CDs and DVDs, nothing more really needs to be said here, but it is another alternative. In the days before cloud backup services and external hard drives I backed up everything to CDs and DVDs. Today, quite honestly, it would just take too much time and be more expensive to go this route. But you can never be too careful so it can add to your backup strategy.

Photo Books

At the end of each year I make a family yearbook containing the year's best photos and memories. The best part is that most photo book services come with hundreds of templates and designs so all I have to do it upload my pictures, then drag and drop them into the template.

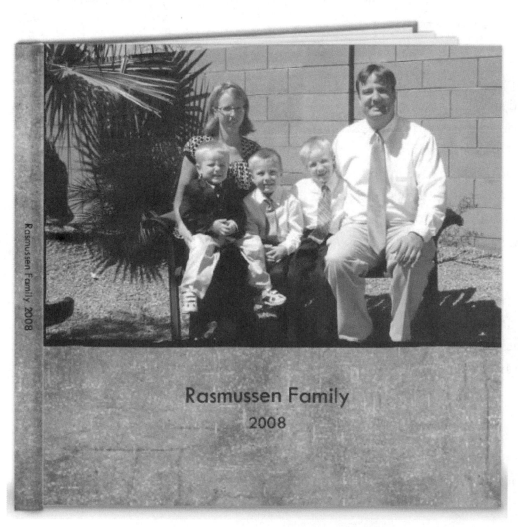

I usually order one 12x12 copy, one 8x8 copy for each of my kids (they will have a whole collection of yearbooks by the time they leave home), and a copy for each set of grandparents. Not only do they make a great gift, but they also serve as yet another backup – not of everything, but at least the kids have something physical they can look at. There's nothing like turning the pages of an actual book, right?

Here are a few sites that create photo books:

- Shutterfly.com
- Picaboo.com
- CreativeMemories.com
- Snapfish.com

Conclusion

So there you have it! You are now armed with the right techniques (and a few tips too!) to be successful in digitizing, editing, preserving, organizing, sharing your digital media collections and backing up. Here is your one-page summary of guidelines.

- A digital image is made up of pixels.
- Before scanning or snapping pictures, set your resolution to between 300-600 dpi.
- Save the original digital image as a TIF or, if you choose JPG, only make edits to a copy of the original.
- Only make edits to a copy of the original digital image.
- Organize your digital media collections using photo management software such as Photoshop Elements, Picasa, Heritage Collector Suite, or others – you cannot be efficiently organized with only a folder system.
- Share your media via printing/mailing, emailing, dropbox, CDs and DVDs, or online via cloud technology.
- Backup, backup, backup!

And remember – life is short, do genealogy first!

Index